YORK NOTES

ATONEMENT

IAN McEWAN

NOTES BY ANNE ROONEY

 Longman

 York Press

The right of Anne Rooney to be identified as Author of this Work
has been asserted by her in accordance with the
Copyright, Designs and Patents Act 1988

YORK PRESS
322 Old Brompton Road, London SW5 9JH

PEARSON EDUCATION LIMITED
Edinburgh Gate, Harlow,
Essex CM20 2JE, United Kingdom
Associated companies, branches and representatives throughout the world

First published 2006

10 9 8 7 6 5 4 3 2 1

ISBN–10: 1–405–83561–3
ISBN–13: 978–1–405–83561–9

Phototypeset by Pantek Arts Ltd, Maidstone, Kent
Printed in China

The author and publisher would like to thank Dr Kate Perry, Dr Alasdair Coles and
Dr Robin Walker of the University of Cambridge and Nicolas Kinloch, Deputy President
of the Historical Association, for their contribution to these Notes

CONTENTS

PART FIVE

BACKGROUND

PART ONE

INTRODUCTION

HOW TO STUDY A NOVEL

Studying a novel on your own requires self-discipline and a carefully thought-out work plan in order to be effective.

- You will need to read the novel more than once. Start by reading it quickly for pleasure, then read it slowly and thoroughly.

- On your second reading make detailed notes on the plot, characters and themes of the novel. Further readings will generate new ideas and help you to memorise the details of the story.

- Some of the characters will develop as the plot unfolds. How do your responses towards them change during the course of the novel?

- Think about how the novel is narrated. From whose point of view are events described?

- A novel may or may not present events chronologically: the time scheme may be a key to its structure and organisation.

- What part do the settings play in the novel?

- Are words, images or incidents repeated so as to give the work a pattern? Do such patterns help you to understand the novel's themes?

- Identify what styles of language are used in the novel.

- What is the effect of the novel's ending? Is the action completed and closed, or left incomplete and open?

- Does the novel present a moral and just world?

- Cite exact sources for all quotations, whether from the text itself or from critical commentaries. Wherever possible find your own examples from the novel to back up your opinions.

- Always express your ideas in your own words.

These York Notes offer an introduction to *Atonement* and cannot substitute for close reading of the text and the study of secondary sources.

CHECK THE BOOK

Malcolm Bradbury's book *The Modern English Novel* (Secker & Warburg, 1993) is a good introduction to the novels of the late twentieth century.

READING *ATONEMENT*

Atonement is a **historical novel** in that most of the action is set in the past. A great many historical novels have been written over time, set in historical periods ranging from the Stone Age to very recent history. Excepting the modern day epilogue to the novel, *Atonement* is set during, and just before, the Second World War, its action taking place in 1935 and 1940. It also has elements of many other literary forms and traditions which are discussed in **Literary background**.

Many historical novels can be described as **popular fiction**, with few aspirations to literary sophistication. In popular historical novels, the setting is often chosen to produce a sense of romance, adventure and excitement, to aid the creation of an escapist fantasy world. *Atonement* does not use its historical setting in this way. Instead, the time in which it is set is vital to the unfolding of the action. The situation of the Second World War, the social attitudes then prevalent and the state of forensic science are all essential to how the tale turns out. It is unlikely that, given the same events, a similar outcome would result if the action took place in 2005.

Literature that endures and remains enjoyable and relevant over years or even centuries always contains an account of experience that is common to people from different cultures. It examines themes such as death, love, loss, personal development and ambition, all of which are unchanging parts of the human condition. Historical fiction relies on these unchanging features of being human for its power. It reassures us that people have always been the same, helps us to **identify** with others in different cultural contexts and endorses our own experiences. But it must also be rooted in the period in which it is set, observing the different social conditions and customs of the time and showing how they affect people and events. In *Atonement*, it is the impact of these social conditions and customs, and of the very particular event of the Second World War, that determines the outcome. The feelings, actions, hopes and fears of the **characters** could be the same in any time and place, but the circumstances in which they are set largely determine what happens.

The **narrator** of *Atonement* is Briony Tallis, who is a young girl for the main part of the action but in telling the story is looking back on events in old age. The novel is the product of Briony's atonement for an act she committed as a child. She has spent most of her life trying to deal with her guilt by writing and re-writing the story of what happened. It is therefore a **reflexive novel** – the writing of it is its own subject.

Even though novels which reflect on the process of their own writing are not especially uncommon, they present particular challenges for the reader. *Atonement* goes further than many in including a long passage of detailed criticism about an earlier version of the story. This is in the form of the letter to Briony from 'CC' (the famous critic, Cyril Connolly, we presume) on her story *Two Figures by a Fountain*. The elderly Briony, too, comments on how she has drafted and re-drafted the story, on the efforts she has made to achieve historical accuracy, and on some mistakes which she has removed. These remarks make us look more closely at the writing and the historical details that remain. Are the details accurate? If not, is there a reason for them to be wrong? Which elements of the beginning part of the novel might have been retained from an early draft? Which parts meet the criticisms offered by Connolly? The novel cannot be read complacently; as McEwan examines the process of writing, so we need to examine the process of our own reading and our relationship to the narrator and the novelist.

As we would expect in a novel which looks directly at the process of its own composition, there is a lot in *Atonement* about writing, imagination, memory, the past, the nature of the truth and the role of literature. There are very frequent references to other works and writers, and there are also **allusions** to books and writers that are not named. It is not necessary to recognise all of these, though a knowledge of some enriches a reading of *Atonement*.

Briony does not reveal herself as the ultimate narrator until the very end of the book. This forces us into a re-evaluation of all we have read and thought up to this point, and is very unsettling on a first reading. Before that, we hear several voices describing events from their own points of view. The voice of Briony as a child, and later as a young adult; the voices of Cecilia and Robbie, the two lovers at the centre of the action; Briony's mother Emily; and, to a

 CHECK THE BOOK

The novel *The French Lieutenant's Woman* (1969) by John Fowles is another novel which combines traditional story-telling with experimental narrative techniques. It, too, has two possible endings – one with the lovers united and one with them irrevocably separated. A film of *The French Lieutenant's Woman* came out in 1981.

lesser extent, two army comrades of Robbie's, all contribute. Their accounts are filtered through Briony's interpretations, though we are not aware of this until the end of the novel. As Briony has proved to be an unreliable witness, and finally to be suffering the early stages of dementia, we are left with a very fluid idea of what happened, how it happened and what, if anything, it all means.

Atonement is challenging, too, in its deeply distressing depictions of the violence and horrors of battle. It is not a novel for the faint-hearted. McEwan makes no attempt to hide the terrors of war, but presents an unrelenting stream of images of injury and distress that leave us reeling. The depiction of war in art of all kinds has a long history, and in many cases the heroism of the brave is glorified at the expense of communicating the terrible reality of what happens to most ordinary people. McEwan rejects any kind of glorification. On the road to Dunkirk, and later in the hospital where Briony works, we are brought face to face with what war does to people, to human bodies and lives. The book does not overtly question the morality of this particular war or of war in general – any questions raised are our own response to what the novel presents.

The novel demands active involvement from its readers, not just in encouraging us to ask questions like this, but even in deciding 'what happens' in the novel. Are we to accept the ending which Briony has chosen to impose on events in the story or take the apparently 'true' ending outlined in the epilogue? In common with much literary fiction from the second half of the twentieth century, *Atonement* requires that we as readers participate in making the reality of the novel. It is challenging, and at times frustrating, but the effort is rewarded by enhanced understanding of our own views on some of the novel's key concerns.

CHECK THE BOOK

Violence and horror have been a feature of much of McEwan's work. Closest to *Atonement* in its realisation of the physicality of the human body is *The Innocent* (1990), in which the central two characters cut up the corpse of a man they have murdered.

PART TWO

THE TEXT

NOTE ON THE TEXT

Atonement was first published in 2001 by Jonathan Cape, London, a subsidiary of Random House. Paperback editions include the Vintage Future Classics edition, also published by Random House, in 2002 and used in the preparation of these Notes. There are large print and audio versions available.

Atonement has been translated into French, German, Spanish, Catalan, Brazilian, Portuguese, Lithuanian and Japanese. It has won The People's Booker Prize (2001), the W. H. Smith Literary Prize, the National Book Critics Circle Award, the Los Angeles Times Prize for Fiction, and the Santiago Prize for the European Novel.

SYNOPSIS

Atonement is divided into three parts and an epilogue. The first part, taking up half of the book, is set on the hottest day of 1935 on the English country estate of the Tallis family. The Tallises' mannered life is depicted at length in a slow-moving portrait of the day. Thirteen-year-old Briony Tallis is trying to produce a **melodrama** she has written, with parts performed by her three visiting cousins. She gives up on this, after witnessing through a window an incident between her sister, Cecilia, and Robbie Turner, the son of the cleaner at the house. The two have been at Cambridge University and have just ended their degrees; there is some awkwardness between them. Briony witnesses Cecilia strip off her clothes and plunge into the fountain in the grounds of their house, watched by Robbie. Unaware that Cecilia dived in to retrieve some pieces from a valuable vase she and Robbie had just broken, Briony does not understand what she sees.

Cecilia's brother, Leon, is returning to the house with a visiting friend, Paul Marshall. This is the occasion for Briony's play.

Robbie, realising he is attracted to Cecilia, writes her a note, then adds an obscene ending. He rewrites it, but puts the wrong version

CHECK THE BOOK

At the start of *Atonement*, Ian McEwan includes a quote from Jane Austen's (1775–1817) novel *Northanger Abbey*. The heroine, Catherine Morland, is an avid reader of Gothic novels, and like Briony, has difficulty in observing the boundaries between reality and fiction. She comes to believe that the inhabitants of Northanger Abbey hide a dreadful secret and that terrible deeds have been committed there. In the quotation, Catherine is reprimanded for allowing her imagination to run wild in this way. McEwan has sometimes referred to *Atonement* as his 'Jane Austen novel'.

SYNOPSIS

CONTEXT

Melodrama became popular in the Victorian era, but began with the plays of the German playwright August von Kotzebue. Typically, the melodramas of the late nineteenth century feature wicked villains who trick and deceive innocent young women. Characters tend to be uncomplicated – either impossibly good or impossibly evil. There are terrible deeds of cruelty, narrow escapes and unashamed sensationalism. Many melodramas are characterised by ill-concealed eroticism in the abusive treatment of the women characters.

CHECK THE BOOK

Another novel set in a country house in a hot summer, involving a child's misunderstanding of an adult sexual relationship, is L. P. Hartley's *The Go-Between* (1953).

into the envelope. He meets Briony on his way to the house for dinner, and gives her the obscene note to carry ahead to Cecilia. Briony opens it and reads it, and is horrified at what she finds. She passes the note to Cecilia, who realises her sister has read it. On the way from her room to dinner, Briony chances to go into the library, where Cecilia and Robbie are making love. Misinterpreting again, she assumes Robbie was attacking her sister and is a dangerous madman. After an awkward dinner, two of the cousins, twin boys, go out of the room, leaving a note to say they have run away. The party breaks up to search for them.

Briony goes to the island in the lake, where she finds her other cousin, Lola, with a man just leaving her. It appears that Lola has been attacked, and Briony quickly convinces herself that Robbie is the rapist. Lola does not deny this. When Robbie returns from the hunt for the twins, having found both of them, he is arrested. He is eventually imprisoned for the rape.

The second part of the novel is set five years later in northern France during the retreat of the British army to Dunkirk. Robbie and two corporals, Nettle and Mace, are making their way to the beach for the evacuation. As they pass through the French countryside, witnessing the horrors of war and being caught in repeated German air attacks, we learn what has happened in the intervening years. Robbie has served part of his sentence and been released to join the armed forces. He and Cecilia are still in love, but have maintained their relationship by letter as she has not be able to visit him. Cecilia has severed all links with her family because they would not accept Robbie's innocence. Briony has at last offered to retract her original statement and admit publicly that Robbie is innocent.

Robbie has a wound in his side, which is infected and becomes progressively worse during the walk to Dunkirk. His mind wanders and he is sometimes delirious. This part of the novel ends with Robbie sleeping in the cellar of a house in Dunkirk the night before the evacuation from the beaches.

The third part of the novel also takes place in the summer of 1940 and is set in England. Briony has become a trainee nurse and is working in a London hospital. Within a few days, the hospital is transformed when the wounded from Dunkirk begin to arrive on the wards. The influx of men with horrendous injuries demands a lot of Briony, but she rapidly develops the skills to deal with them and to handle the trauma of caring for them.

Briony's ambition to be a writer has continued and she has sent a story based around the episode at the fountain to a literary journal. The journal rejects her story, but with an encouraging letter that gives an extended critique of her writing. The story is an early version of the first part of the novel.

Briony learns in a letter from her family that Paul Marshall and Lola are to marry, and goes to the church, uninvited, to watch the small wedding. After the service, she goes to Cecilia's flat. Cecilia is shocked by her arrival and their meeting is very fraught and tense. Cecilia remains hostile and resentful towards Briony. Robbie, who is also in the flat, finds it hard to keep control of his fury. Cecilia and Robbie are both surprised to learn from Briony that she is now certain that Paul committed the rape, and are shocked and angered to hear of Paul and Lola's marriage. The marriage means that it will not be possible to bring Paul to justice as Lola will not speak against him. At the end of the meeting, Robbie makes Briony promise to swear a legal oath, to tell her parents the truth and to write a full account of what really happened. This account will become *Atonement*.

In a final epilogue written by Briony in 1999, we learn that the novel is the culmination of a series of drafts she has created during her life, her act of atonement. Some of the characters seen earlier are still alive. Briony sees from a distance Paul and Lola, now Lord and Lady Marshall, when she visits the Imperial War Museum to deposit letters she has used in writing her book. She acknowledges that her book cannot be published until Paul and Lola are dead, which will be after her own death. She attends a party for her birthday held in the old Tallis family home, now a country house hotel, where her melodrama is finally performed.

Briony has been diagnosed with a form of dementia, and her memory and other faculties will slowly deteriorate until eventually

CHECK THE BOOK

What Maisie Knew (1897) by Henry James is another novel which presents the main action from the point of view of a child.

she dies. This means that the current version of the story is the last she can ever write. She reveals that it is the first version in which she has had Cecilia and Robbie alive and together at the end. In all previous versions she followed the true pattern of events, which, she suggests, saw them both dead before the end of 1940.

DETAILED SUMMARIES

PART ONE

CHAPTER 1

- Briony Tallis has written a play which she intends to perform with her cousins for her older brother Leon on his return home to their country estate.
- Briony has a passion for writing and considers herself to have talent and promise.
- Her cousins, fifteen-year-old Lola and twins Pierrot and Jackson, are refugees from a broken home who will be staying in the Tallis household while their feckless mother is in Paris with a new lover.
- The rehearsals for the play quickly disappoint and frustrate Briony as Lola takes the lead role which Briony had written for herself and the boys prove at first reluctant and then inept.

CHECK THE FILM

One of the most famous melodramas, based on a real event, was written anonymously in the nineteenth century and titled, *Maria Martin, or Murder in the Red Barn*. It was made into a film by Milton Rosmer in 1935.

The novel opens with Briony Tallis, youngest daughter of a civil servant father and a semi-invalid mother, awaiting the arrival of visiting cousins and her older brother. The family lives in a solid, large house in the English countryside with servants and land. It is a very hot day in the summer of 1935.

Briony has written a play – a **melodrama** – which she intends to perform with her three cousins to impress her brother. She has previously written stories which she has shared with her family. Her parents, sister and brother have indulgently praised and encouraged her work and Briony revels in what she sees as her success as a writer. She experiments with new words she reads in a dictionary and thesaurus, and examples of her inexpert use of these is given, inviting us to laugh gently at her.

Briony's real life is uneventful and isolated. She doesn't have any secrets, or anyone to keep secrets from, although she would like to have. Instead, she pours her energies into writing and imagining. This thirst for real drama in her life will shape later events.

As soon as her cousins arrive, Briony tries to drag them off to rehearse her play, but Briony's mother, Emily, and elder sister, Cecilia, intervene to give the cousins a gentler welcome. By late afternoon, all four children are in the library and Briony struggles to get the twin boys interested in her project. Briony has assumed she will have the lead role, but ends up giving this to Lola and resenting it. Lola tries to behave as much like an adult as she can. This is threatening and confusing to the younger Briony who does not always know how to respond to her. The twins are not capable of saying their lines in the dramatic style that Briony would like, and the chapter ends on a tense note as they are 'steadily wrecking Briony's creation' (p. 17) until called away for a bath.

COMMENTARY

Although events are related by an anonymous, third person narrator, the voice in many passages is that of Briony. She is the central character of the early part of the book and the one who will seek the 'atonement' of the title. Only at the very end of the book do we discover that the whole story is being told by the older Briony.

We see hints of Briony's literary ambition immediately in phrases such as 'a two-day tempest of composition' and 'the distant north' (p. 3), the latter a cliché from the type of children's books she would have spent hours reading. The style which characterises the passages presented from Briony's point of view is self-regarding, ostentatiously 'literary' and often flamboyant. By the end of the first page, the full, extravagant extent of her literary pretensions has been laid bare in the outline of the melodrama, *The Trials of Arabella*, she has written. Her active imagination is demonstrated again as she fantasises about the effect the play will have on her brother – as far as guiding him to choose a suitable bride who would make Briony her bridesmaid.

CHECK THE FILM

Although melodrama was at its popular height in the Victorian era, by the 1930s a genre of film known as 'the weepies' was taking cinema audiences by storm. These films were specifically aimed at women and had strong, female protagonists. Stars included Marlene Dietrich and Greta Garbo, famous for their respective roles in *The Devil is a Woman* (1935) and *Anna Karenina* (1935).

The performance is not to take place, however. In slipping out of Briony's young voice and telling us in advance that the play will not reach fulfilment, McEwan breaks the chronological flow of the **narrative** and frustrates our natural keenness to see what will happen. At many key points in the novel, and several minor ones like this, we are told how things will turn out. This undermines **dramatic tension** but has the effect of forcing us to focus on how events and characters affect one another. As we already know what will happen, we turn our attention to how it will happen. How events lead to one another and why events turn out as they do are major concerns of the book.

Briony's character is developed considerably as we hear about her writing, her liking for order, and her desire for secrets. As much about her personality is conveyed in the use of language, which copies Briony's own vocabulary, as in the relation of, and commentary on, events.

One cryptic line offers a suggestion of how later events might be understood. We are told that Briony's lack of opportunity to hide real secrets was not 'particularly an affliction; or rather, it appeared so only in retrospect, once a solution had been found' (p. 5). The one secret which comes to dominate and ruin the lives of the central characters is casually signposted here as 'a solution' to the problem of Briony having nothing to hide.

Her melodrama, we are told, was intended to 'inspire ... terror, relief and instruction, in that order' (p. 8). This is an **allusion** to Aristotle's *Poetics*, a critical text on writing drama composed in Athens during the fourth century BC. Aristotle says that the nature of **tragedy** is to inspire terror and pity in the safe environment of the theatre and then to relieve them in the drama's **resolution**. The question of whether literature has a duty of instruction also has a long history.

The narrator keeps some emotional distance between herself (and therefore us) and the young Briony. We are given opportunities to laugh at Briony, to enjoy our own superior knowledge of vocabulary, literary forms, and the actions and motivation of adolescent girls. We are told that she has probably never heard of

CONTEXT

Tragedy and melodrama are very different. In a tragedy, a hero of epic stature is brought from a high status to death through a reversal of fortune. There is no place for sentiment, random misfortune or motiveless actions. His fall is caused by a 'fatal flaw' in his character which means his response to events leads to his downfall. It is important that the hero recognises how his own failings have caused his doom. The action must be consistent and complete, and not depend on anything outside the scope of the tragedy.

melodrama, but at the same time we are expected to recognise the allusion to scholarly debates about literature.

At one point the narrator lays claim to uncertainty about Briony's inner state – 'Perhaps she herself was struggling with the temptation to flounce from the room' (p. 16). On one level, this is clearly a **conceit** – McEwan knows what he intends Briony's thoughts and feelings to be. But it also acknowledges that once created a story and its characters take on lives of their own, beyond the author's intentions – a fact that escapes the young Briony, who seeks to control every aspect of her creation.

The opening chapter is used largely to introduce Briony and her literary ambitions, though the action gets underway (for us and Briony) once the cousins arrive. It is a slow and languorous start to the novel, and sets up the feeling that 'not much happens' which is sustained throughout most of Part One.

 CHECK THE NET
For information on Aristotle's theory of tragedy, go to **www.en.wikipedia. org** and type 'Poetics' into the search engine.

 QUESTION
Briony says that there is nothing she cannot describe. It has been said that 'this ability to describe, to fashion the world in words, is both Briony's gift and her curse'. To what extent is this true?

CONTEXT
When Briony uses cholera as the illness her heroine is suffering from she may have been thinking of the respiratory disease consumption (tuberculosis). This is more commonly used as an illness in melodrama and has romantic associations. Victims have pale skin with very rosy cheeks.

GLOSSARY

3	**cholera** acute illness causing vomiting, abdominal pain and diarrhoea.
5	**corralled** driven into a corrall – an enclosure for animals (usually horses or cattle rather than hens)
5	**fool's gold** the yellow mineral pyrite, which is often mistaken for gold
5	**cryptographic system** code
6	**esoteric** obscure or out of the ordinary, often only understood by one particular group
6	**hoodlum** lawless youth or petty gangster
6	**shameless auto-exculpation** exculpate is to free or liberate from blame, and 'auto' used as a prefix means 'relating to the self'. There is a pun on 'auto' meaning car as well as 'self'
6	**cursory** here, brief or hasty. Briony is using the word in the wrong sense, as it usually has the meaning 'superficial'. There is an element of a pun, as the origin of the word is in the Latin *cursus*, a course, from *currerre*, to run
7	**Quintus Tertullian** (c. 155–230 AD) early Christian writer who lived in Carthage (now Tunisia) and wrote the first important Christian works in Latin

PART ONE CHAPTER 1 continued

CONTEXT
Rabindranath Tagore (1861–1941) (p. 7) was an Indian writer and poet who shot to fame in the West in 1912 after he translated his own work from Bengali into English. He was championed by the poet W. B. Yeats, and received the Nobel Prize for Literature in 1913, the first non-Westerner to do so.

CONTEXT
The 'Abyssinia Question' Briony dismisses on p. 9 was a topical issue in 1935. The League of Nations' failure to protect Abyssinia from invasion by Mussolini's Italy led to a crisis. Hitler sent troops to help the Abyssinians and so distracted attention from Germany's re-armament and ambitions to expand in Europe, ultimately leading to the Second World War.

GLOSSARY CONTINUED

7   nuptials marriage celebrations

9   dastardly antithesis mean and cowardly opposite; 'dastardly' has connotations of melodrama as it was often used of the villain

9   mendacity untruthfulness

9   re-armament Germany's acquisition and stock-piling of arms after the end of the First World War. The Treaty of Versailles in 1919 limited the military force Germany was allowed to keep

CHAPTER 2

- Cecilia Tallis, Briony's sister, has picked flowers for the guest room.
- She takes a valuable vase with an important family history to fill with water at a fountain in the garden and runs into Robbie, the son of the cleaning lady.
- Relations between the pair are strained. As Cecilia rejects Robbie's offer of help with filling the vase, they break the vase and two fragments fall to the bottom of the fountain.
- Again refusing Robbie's help, Cecilia undresses and retrieves the fragments, then stalks into the house.

Cecilia has been asked by her mother to put flowers in the guest bedroom for Paul Marshall. She avoids talking to Robbie, the son of the family's cleaning lady, who is working in the garden. Robbie has been educated at the Tallises' expense and treated like a member of the family since his father's disappearance many years ago. Relations between Cecilia and Robbie have become strained since they both went to Cambridge University.

Cecilia goes into the house, where she arranges the flowers in a valuable vase with a dramatic family history. The vase had been presented to her father's brother Clem as a token of gratitude by a

French village that he had helped to liberate during the First World War.

Cecilia takes the vase outside to fill it at the fountain. She has an awkward discussion with Robbie about literature and his plans to become a doctor. Robbie offers to help Cecilia fill the vase with water, but she refuses. He persists, and between them they break off part of the rim, the fragments falling into the bottom of the fountain. Cecilia punishes Robbie by silently undressing and plunging into the freezing water to retrieve the pieces, then stalking back to the house without speaking to him.

COMMENTARY

The narratorial voice has changed for this chapter, and we observe events from Cecilia's point of view. Her voice comes through quite clearly, as she describes everything in the scene with a precision and care that make it possible to visualise it exactly. She carefully observes not just her surroundings but herself in them. Cecilia describes events and scenery as though she is imagining how her description will be judged, and places herself in the scene with a keen awareness of how she appears to Robbie as well as to readers.

The extensive description makes the chapter move very slowly. Time is expended on recounting and analysing the smallest details. This contributes to the languid, even sluggish, air of the hot summer day. Cecilia tries to break out of this languor herself, by running, by plunging into cold water, by refreshing the flowers – but her slow prose always undermines these attempts.

The only event in this chapter is the breaking of the vase. By explaining its history, Cecilia gives the vase something of a mythical status. The build up makes the accident more dramatic, and Cecilia's carefully calculated response milks it for every last bit of impact. She chooses her own actions to make Robbie feel as bad as possible, revelling in his distress and reiterating that it is his 'punishment' every time she thinks of another way of making him uncomfortable. In her

> **CONTEXT**
>
> This was the first part of the novel that McEwan wrote. He once explained in an interview: 'After about 15 months, I found I'd written a couple of paragraphs which I knew had taken me into the novel I was going to write. And it was just this girl stepping into the room with a bunch of wildflowers.'

> **CONTEXT**
>
> The Triton fountain in Piazza Barberini, which the Tallises' fountain is based on, was designed by Bernini in 1643. There is a dark side to its history – until the late eighteenth century, unidentified dead bodies were displayed in front of it, and the people of Rome invited to try to recognise them.

CONTEXT

Meissen is a fine porcelain from the town of Meissen in Germany, first made in 1710. Johann Gregor Höroldt (1696–1775) introduced the style of Chinoiserie and new pigments with vivid colours when he was in charge of the painting department at the Meissen factory around 1720.

final, ludicrous, 'Drowning herself would be his punishment' (p. 30), we glimpse something of her sister Briony's over-dramatisation.

Later events will make the drama of the broken vase look absurd, but here its importance is easily exaggerated as nothing else is happening.

Although the events of the chapter are slight, there is turmoil beneath the surface and this is the first glimpse we have of the relationship between Robbie and Cecilia which will be so important in the novel. We see this only from Cecilia's point of view here, and as she struggles to find reasons for the awkwardness between them we can't help feeling that she is avoiding confronting the obvious – that it is the attraction between them that makes them nervous in each other's presence. Her assumption that Robbie is unsettled by the difference in their social stations is rather ridiculous and says more about her snobbishness than about him. She is embarrassed that he has done better than her at Cambridge, and experiments with the possibility that this has made him arrogant. Her unwillingness to be drawn into a literary discussion might hint that she is aware of his superior intellect. Cecilia's fear that she has suggested 'a taste for the full-blooded and sensual' (p. 25) in her preference for Fielding over Richardson is the closest she comes to acknowledging the sexual tension between them.

CONTEXT

When Cecilia identifies her room with 'stews' on p. 21, she may just mean that the room is a slovenly mess, but she would have been aware of Shakespeare's use of the word to mean a brothel.

GLOSSARY

18	**kissing gate** a gate set in a U- or V-shape so that only one person can pass through at a time
18	**ha-ha** wall set in a ditch to divide up land without intruding into the landscape
18	**Triton** Greek sea god with a man's upper body and a fish's tail in place of legs
19	**rugosa** a woody shrub rose with informal appearance, floppy single or double flowers and a strong, sweet scent
19	**coming down** leaving the University of Cambridge after completing a degree

GLOSSARY CONTINUED

19   **Pevsner** Sir Nikolaus Pevsner (1902–83), British
      architectural historian and author of *Buildings of
      England* (1951–74) which describes every notable
      building in the country

19   **Adam-style** after the style of Scottish architect Robert
      Adam (1728–92), who copied the styles of the Italian
      Renaissance. McEwan's boarding school, Woolverston, was
      another Adam-style building

19   **stuccoed** decorated with mouldings made from stucco – a
      weather-resistant mix of dehydrated lime, crushed marble
      and glue

19   **Friesians** a type of black and white cow giving a high milk
      yield

20   **rose-bay willow-herb** wild plant with tall spikes of pink
      flowers

20   **Chesterfield** large, well-stuffed sofa with arms the same
      height as the back

22   **first** first class degree, the highest class of degree

24   **Victoria and Albert** museum in South Kensington, London,
      which houses art objects from around the world

24   **King August** Augustus the Strong, Elector of Saxony and
      King of Poland (1670–1733). Augustus imprisoned an
      alchemist, Johann Frederick Bottger, and charged him with
      finding out how to make porcelain. He later moved him to
      his palace at Meissen

24   **Chinoiserie** style of design featuring imitations of Chinese
      figures and motifs

24   **Sotheby's** famous auction house based in London, which
      deals principally in antiques and fine art

25   **Bolshevik** Russian communist party led by Vladimir Lenin,
      which took power in Russia after the October Revolution
      in 1917

28   **patina** film formed over the surface of something

29   **arcanists** people who tried to discover the secret of
      making porcelain. The formula for porcelain was referred
      to as the 'arcanum' and was kept secret by the Chinese
      porcelain makers

**CHECK
THE BOOK**

Clarissa (p. 25) is a
novel in seven
volumes by the
writer Samuel
Richardson
(1689–1761),
published in 1747–8.
The story is
presented in the
form of letters
between four
characters and tells
of the heroine's
seduction and rape
by a disreputable
suitor followed by
her retreat into
solitude and final
death from shame
and guilt. It is the
longest novel in
English.

CONTEXT

The novelist and
playwright Henry
Fielding (1707–54)
wrote boisterous
and sensual novels
about the (often
bawdy) exploits of
London characters.
Some of Fielding's
novels are
parodies of
Richardson's more
serious works.

CHAPTER 3

- Briony struggles to get her cousins to rehearse the play.
- In a pause in rehearsals, Briony witnesses through the window the scene between Cecilia and Robbie at the fountain. She misinterprets the action.
- Briony feels the urge to write an account of what she has seen, but realises she has a duty to continue rehearsals instead.

One of the twins, Jackson, has wet the bed and is having to wash his sheets in the laundry, preventing him from rehearsing. Briony, meanwhile, struggles with Pierrot's inability to intone his lines convincingly and Lola's distance. She fears that Lola thinks her childish and is only indulging her.

Left alone for a while, Briony plays at flexing her fingers and wondering about the gap between thought and action, and whether other people have as full a consciousness as she does herself. She concludes that they probably do, but finds the implications of this quite alarming. She then decides that she should have written a story and not a play, since a play is mediated through actors who can destroy her work.

Looking from the window, she sees Cecilia and Robbie. The scene from the previous chapter is played out again, this time silently, and Briony misinterprets what she is seeing. At first, she expects a proposal of marriage, then she assumes that Robbie is commanding Cecilia to undress. She reflects on what she has seen, trying to take a grown-up, detached view of it and move away from the childish view that it was somehow acted out for her benefit. She wants to write about what she has seen, and imagines presenting three different points of view and versions of the action – her own, Robbie's and Cecilia's.

COMMENTARY

Briony's voice is used to reveal more of her character. She flits between an adolescent and a childish view and behaviour, at one moment reflecting that it is immature not to take more care of her

? **QUESTION** This is the first of Briony's several misinterpretations of what she sees. What other instances of mistaken seeing are there in *Atonement*?

appearance and a little later wiping her dirty hands on her white muslin dress. She is child-like as she plays with her fingers, yet more mature in her consideration of other people's minds. She recognises in herself a childish impulse to see the scene between Cecilia and Robbie as carrying some meaning for her. A moment later she is quite grown-up in her acknowledgment that the scene has no meaning outside its actions, and would have taken place whether or not she were observing it. This retreat from seeing herself as the point or centre of the scene echoes the gradual recognition a child has that it is not, in fact, the centre of the universe for everyone else. She thinks about what it must be like to be someone else. This imaginative projection – the ability fully to imagine what it is like to be another person – is an essential skill for a writer. There is more on this passage in the **Extended commentaries**.

Briony attempts to interpret the action she sees through the window, attributing thoughts and motives to Robbie and Cecilia, but gets it horribly wrong. It is with some **irony** that she observes 'how easy it was to get everything wrong, completely wrong' (p. 39).

Briony sees everything as material for her writing, and immediately ponders what use she can make of the scene she has witnessed. She reflects that there is no absolute meaning in an event, but only what it means to different people. If this is perhaps too advanced a notion for the character we see flitting between adolescence and childhood, an excuse is provided almost immediately as the **narrative** viewpoint draws back and we are invited to reflect on the episode from six decades in the future, with the old Briony admitting that she cannot disentangle what she thought as a child from what she has thought or written since. The narrative is instantly undermined, and another layer of uncertainty about what actually happened, and what it meant, is added.

As Briony stands considering that she could write a scene like the one she has just witnessed, we feel a strange lurch as we realise we are in fact reading the account she has just planned to write, and are caught up in a **reflexive**, distorted sequence. On a first reading, we are unlikely to be aware of this dislocation, but on subsequent readings it prepares the ground for a sequence of points in the novel in which the ground seems to shift under our feet. Here, the older

> **CONTEXT**
>
> Briony's consideration of other people's consciousness is a contemplation of the theory of mind. This is the recognition that other people have a mind of their own, which resembles our own in many respects but is essentially distinct, and filled with their own thoughts, feelings and concerns.

CONTEXT

The poet Samuel Taylor Coleridge (1772–1834) wrote in *Biographia Literaria* (1817) of the 'willing suspension of disbelief' that allows us to believe in a fiction or poem. We know that a story is not literally 'true' but agree to believe in it to enjoy it and receive its message. McEwan abuses the reader's trust by exploiting the suspension of disbelief – encouraging us to believe in the fiction and then underlining the fact that it is a fiction.

Briony is writing about the younger Briony imagining writing the scene that the older Briony has just written. This playing with the narratorial point of view and the **conceit** of composition engages us intellectually, disturbing the emotional engagement we are building with the voice of the young Briony. Early instances of undermining our voluntary belief in the fiction, such as this, lay the foundations for the whole-scale demolition of the literary edifice at the end of the novel. We may feel frustrated and cheated by this, as we feel we have entered into a contract with the author who is now reneging on the bargain by stepping back from a fiction that we have been led to believe in.

GLOSSARY

40   Bakelite   hard, brittle plastic resin used in the first half of the twentieth century

CHAPTER 4

- Briony tears down the poster for the melodrama, deciding not to go ahead with the performance.
- Leon Tallis arrives, with his guest Paul Marshall. On the way to the house he encounters Robbie and invites him to dinner.
- Cecilia is annoyed with Leon and wants him to rescind the invitation.
- Leon and Cecilia quickly re-establish the balance of conspiracy and antagonism that marked their childhood relationship.

Cecilia has successfully repaired the vase so that barely-visible cracks are the only evidence of the accident. In the hallway, she meets Briony who has clearly been crying. Briony dramatically tears down her poster but refuses to be consoled, wandering outside barefoot and making her way towards the island in the lake. Cecilia takes the flowers to Paul Marshall's room and through the window sees Leon and Paul arrive, the horse-drawn trap stopping while Leon talks to Robbie.

Cecilia leads Paul and Leon to the terrace near the swimming pool where they talk – or, rather, where Paul tells them about his confectionery business and its success, and explains his ambitions to make money out of the widely predicted war by selling special 'Amo' bars with camouflage patterned wrappers. Leon and Cecilia exchange the special 'look' that they used as a weapon as children. United by this, they are immediately set at odds by Cecilia's anger on discovering that Leon has invited Robbie to dinner. Leon refuses to cancel the invitation. They retire to the house for a cocktail.

COMMENTARY

This is another chapter related from Cecilia's point of view. Again she notices and describes everything in minute detail, in the very precise, self-conscious style established in Chapter 2.

The opening scene establishes the dynamic between Briony and Cecilia. Briony, tempestuous and dramatic, tears her poster but struggles not to cry, resisting the childishness of tears and cuddles. Cecilia notices with regret the indication that Briony is growing up and changing. When Briony decides to share the reason for her temper with Cecilia, she characteristically chooses a word, 'genre' (p. 45), she has recently learned and mispronounces it so that Cecilia does not understand her. We end up smiling at her childishness rather than recognising her maturity as she had hoped Cecilia would do. This reduction to ridicule is a technique that McEwan frequently uses to undermine Briony's self-conscious seriousness.

It is clear that while Cecilia thinks she is disregarding Robbie, in fact he is constantly intruding into her thoughts. She has 'passed many hours deliberately not thinking of Robbie Turner' (p. 43) and even the furniture, polished by his mother, reminds her of him. Later, her anger that Leon has invited Robbie to dinner emphasises the exaggerated importance he is assuming in her thoughts.

As Briony is embarking on adolescence, Cecilia is leaving it behind, but occasionally reverts to childish patterns of behaviour. She is too afraid of her father to confront him over the issue of smoking, and gives Leon ' "the look" ' (p. 50). She is like a romantic teenager in reflecting as she meets Paul whether she will marry him. The reflection is not straightforward: she wonders if she will look back

> **CONTEXT**
>
> 'Amo' is Latin for 'I love', which is inappropriate as the name of a chocolate bar, but is probably a cynical marketing gimmick. More appositely, Paul intends to produce a version for the army, who will recognise 'amo' as an abbreviation of 'ammunition'.

on this moment later, and imagines a future of happiness or disappointment stemming from it. It is one of many imagined futures in the novel.

Here she sees events as though fixed in the past when she contemplates the appearance of Danny Hardman, the sixteen-year-old son of old Hardman who works on the Tallises' estate. 'All day long ... she had been ... seeing strangely, as though everything was already long in the past, made more vivid by posthumous ironies she could not quite grasp' (p. 48). McEwan uses this technique to alert us to passages and reflections that will have a bearing on later events. In this case, Cecilia's suspicion that Danny is interested in Lola is carried through to her later conviction that he was the one who attacked Lola. Again, at the end of the chapter, she feels that she is seeing everything as though it happened in the past and all outcomes are already fixed.

The **character** of Paul Marshall is introduced and he is not **sympathetic**. He delivers a long speech about himself in which he appears to be self-important, pompous and conceited. Concentrating on his own achievements, particularly as they are in trade and commerce, would have been considered especially rude at the time when the novel is set. Talking about money and commercial success were considered vulgar – a vulgarity recalled later by the appearance of the aged Paul and Lola with their expensive clothes and Lola's vivid make-up.

Paul is pompous and even ridiculous in his view of his chocolate-making as a 'purpose' and 'vision' (p. 50). The accusation of warmongering is also absurd and his repetition of it self-aggrandising. More important than these unpleasant aspects of his character, though, is the suggestion that he touches Cecilia lightly on the arm as they go into the house. She is unsure whether he has done so, and the episode is easy to overlook. But when we learn much later that it was he who assaulted Lola, the unsolicited touch looks more ominous.

GLOSSARY

43	**Chagall** Marc Chagall (1887–1985), Russian-born French painter whose paintings often show several episodes of a narrative sequence dotted around the same canvas
43	**montage** combination of images put together
45	**trap** small horse-drawn cart for passengers
45	**chintz counterpane** bedspread made of a thin printed cotton with a glazed finish. The printed design is often of flowers and leaves
45	**Chippendale sofa** sofa made by, or in the style of, English cabinet maker Thomas Chippendale (1718–79), characterised by Gothic or Chinese motifs, heavy wooden carving and curved wooden legs
46	**trousseau chest** chest used by a bride to contain the collection of clothes and household linen with which she started married life
47	**Whitehall ministry** ministers in the British parliament have their offices in Whitehall, London, where they are staffed by many senior civil servants
47	**anodyne** pleasant but uninspiring
48	**sepia** with a yellowish-brown tint
48	**posthumous ironies** ironic overtones that become evident later
49	**monologue** uninterrupted speech delivered by one character
49	**unions** trade unions – groups of workers acting together to negotiate improved working conditions and pay. Trade unions have been legal in the UK since 1867 and grew in power and influence during the years after the First World War
50	**if Mr Hitler did not pipe down** Adolf Hitler, leader of the Nazis (National Socialist German Workers Party) in Germany. The phrase 'pipe down' meaning to be quiet, and the understatement this conveys, are typical of 1930s upper-class English usage
50	**warmonger** someone who encourages or keenly anticipates war
50	**maligned** spoken badly of, unjustly described
50	**venerable** worthy of being revered or venerated
52	**Roedean** private English girls' school
52	**grammar school** state-funded school attended by pupils who passed a selection test at eleven years old

CONTEXT

By 'sophisticates' (p. 46) McEwan means girls at Girton College, Cambridge, particularly those who thought themselves sophisticated. In 1935, Girton was one of only two Cambridge Colleges to admit women (and not men). Women were not allowed to become full members of the University until 1948.

> **GLOSSARY CONTINUED**
>
> 53   **is he bothering you?** Leon is asking whether Robbie is making sexual advances to Cecilia
>
> 53   **mitigated** reduced in impact
>
> 53   **foreshortened** with the appearance of being shorter than it is because of the angle of view
>
> 53   **infinitesimally** very slightly

CHAPTER 5

- The twins and Lola begin to get homesick and restless.
- Paul Marshall comes upon them as Lola is telling Jackson off for saying their parents are going to get a divorce. He chats to them, and produces an Amo bar from his pocket, which Lola eats.

CONTEXT

Polo (p. 62) is a round mint with a hole in the middle; Aero is a chocolate bar full of bubbles; Oxo is an instant stock cube, available only as beef stock concentrate in 1935; Brillo is a metal scouring pad containing soap. Polos were in fact not introduced until 1948 so the twins could have no experience of them. Aero was introduced in 1935, the year in which the action of Part One takes place.

Briony has not told Lola and the twins that she is cancelling the performance, but simply walks out without comment. They only realise that the rehearsals are ended for good when Lola wanders into Paul Marshall's room and sees Briony walking near the island.

Disappointed, the twins go to Lola's room. They are bored, homesick and hungry. She tries to reassure them, but Jackson says they won't ever go home because their parents are divorcing. Lola is furious with him for saying a word they had all avoided.

Paul Marshall surprises them by speaking from the doorway straight afterwards. In the exchange that follows, Lola acts as maturely as she can, but struggles sometimes to know what she should be saying and doing. She reprimands Paul for saying in front of the twins that he has read about their parents in the press, and Paul is contrite.

Paul brings out an Amo bar, but as the twins contradict his prediction that there will be a war and are rude about the name of the bar, he gives it to Lola. He watches her eat it, until Betty's voice calls the boys to their bath.

COMMENTARY

The action is presented largely from the point of view of Lola, though with insights from the twins and also Paul Marshall. At one point we see action in Paul's room which the other **characters** have not witnessed. Although the older Briony is the ultimate **narrator** here, expressions and views which must belong to the other characters stud the chapter.

Lola's character is developed further, reinforcing what we have seen of her already as a girl on the brink of adulthood who combines childish, adolescent and older attitudes by turns. She adopts the caring role in putting an arm around Jackson when he is unhappy, though the childish thinness of her arm undermines the gesture and makes Jackson all the sadder. She copies what we assume is her mother's behaviour in her angry response to Jackson's blunder in mentioning divorce, and in her words to Paul Marshall: 'Then I'll thank you not to talk about them in front of the children' (p. 59). The counterpoint of adult and child is most pronounced in the history of the trousers. Her story, that she bought them from Liberty's (a sophisticated adult shop) while going to London to see *Hamlet*, sounds like the actions of a grown woman. But behind the story, the reality is that she was at a matinee performance and spilt strawberry drink on her 'frock' (p. 60), so had to go to the nearest shop to buy clean clothes – a very childish scenario.

While adopting what she considers to be adult behaviour and speech, Lola is still very much a child. She flicks open a catch on Paul's suitcase, then closes it and flees. She curls her tongue around the Amo bar and gives the twins a 'serves-you-right look' as any petulant sister would. Furthermore, she panics and struggles to know what to do – has Paul heard the whole exchange about divorce? How should she respond to his comment about the papers?

The mix of adult and child in Lola is apparently interesting to Paul Marshall. He has been dozing in his room, and after a dream in which his younger sisters touch his body, he wakes sexually aroused. This is a disturbing image, which does nothing to improve the poor impression we have of him. As he watches Lola curl her tongue around the Amo bar, the account is sensual and the effect on

> **CONTEXT**
>
> The threat of 'The Parents' (p. 57) has clearly has been used before, hence the capitalisation – it has special meaning and resonance for the children. This meaning is now rendered obsolete by the threat of divorce, as their parents will no longer be a single unit of authority. Divorce was a rare occurrence in 1935 – only 20,056 divorces were granted in England and Wales in the five years between 1931 and 1935, compared with 734,701 in 1996 to 2000. Lola's reluctance to talk about divorce reflects the social stigma attached to it at the time.

CONTEXT

The Pre-Raphaelite Brotherhood, formed in 1848, was a group of seven English painters that included Edward Burne-Jones, John Everett Millais and Dante Gabriel Rossetti. Their paintings are romantic, beautiful and intricate. A favourite model of the group was Lizzie Siddal, who had long, flame-coloured hair. It is therefore to paintings of Lizzie that Paul's thoughts may be turning.

him is unnervingly sexual – 'he took a deep breath. "Bite it," he said softly. "You've got to bite it" ' (p. 62). Uncomfortably, Lola reminds him of his favourite sister (p. 61). The adult/child hybrid that excites him is clear again in the last sentence. With her mouth full of chocolate, Lola adopts the maternal tone again 'Bath time! Run along now. Run along' (p. 62).

GLOSSARY

57	**sibilant** with an 's' sound
57	**totem** symbol
59	**magus** master
60	**Liberty's** Liberty of London, an exclusive and slightly Bohemian department store in London, facing onto Regent Street and Great Marlborough Street, opened in 1875
60	**London Palladium** London theatre in Argyll Street, opposite the Great Marlborough Street entrance to Liberty's
61	**Ducker's in The Turl** Ducker and Son Ltd, gentleman's shoe-makers at 6 Turl Street, Oxford, sometimes said to make the best shoes in the world
62	**Amo amas amat** 'I love, you love, he/she/it loves'

Chapter 6

- Emily Tallis spends the afternoon in her bedroom, in the dark, fearing the onset of a migraine.

- As the threat retreats, she contemplates what is happening in the house, the members of the family, her role in the household and what she will do when she gets up.

- She finally rises, but doesn't yet leave the room.

The first we see of Emily Tallis she is lying in a darkened room hoping to avoid a migraine. The chapter is taken up with her ponderings on her family, her role in it, and her account of how migraine – or the threat of migraine – has affected her life. We learn that she considers herself hampered, almost imprisoned, by the danger of a migraine and that her fear of it has prevented her taking an active part in her family's life.

Finally, she decides that she is not going to succumb on this occasion. She spends some considerable time planning what she will do when she is out of the room, and then delays her emergence further by deciding to search for dark glasses and flat shoes so that she can go outside to look for Briony.

COMMENTARY

Through Emily's own voice, we learn a lot about her **character** in this chapter. It is significant that she has not featured in the book so far – her retreat from the family and the house outside her room is mirrored in her late arrival in the plot. She likes to feel that she is a central, coordinating force, but in fact she appears to be redundant in a household that runs itself without her. Her one clear act so far has been to order a roast dinner, a meal which is highly inappropriate on such a hot day and which is causing strife in the kitchens. The room is almost an extension of herself as she notices the creaks and strains of the building with the same attentiveness she devotes to monitoring the state of her own body, teetering on the brink of a migraine.

She has an indulgent, romantic view of Briony and a sentimental view of herself as mother. She is already nostalgic for the time when Briony was smaller and considers herself to have been at her best and most sparkling when with her. Despite what she says, the history she describes reveals that she has been at best ineffectual, and at worst neglectful, as a mother. She says that she has 'longed to rise up and intervene, especially if she thought Briony was in need of her' (pp. 66–7) but the fear of pain has stood in her way. She lists a string of domestic chores she will carry out ahead of finding and comforting Briony.

She has a low opinion of Cecilia, even though (or perhaps, subconsciously, because) Cecilia seems to manage the household and Briony well. She considers that Cecilia's time at Cambridge was wasted, that it may have made her unmarriageable and has not fitted her for later life. She has the conventional view of a woman of her class at the time – that a woman should devote her life to her husband and children, and academic pursuits are pointless.

<table>
<tr><td>**CONTEXT**</td></tr>
<tr><td>The depiction of Emily's migraine as a prowling animal recalls the writer Samuel Johnson (1709–84), who characterised his depression as a 'black dog'.</td></tr>
</table>

CONTEXT

Upper-class girls were often sent to Switzerland to 'finishing school' where they learned ladylike tasks such how a table should be set for a formal dinner, how to manage servants and the rudiments of topics likely to come up in conversation. Swiss finishing schools were a popular choice as they gave girls a chance to perfect their French.

Emily's view of Paul Marshall is misguided and naïve. Hearing a 'little squeal of laughter, abruptly smothered' (p. 69) she assumes this is innocent activity between Paul and Lola and an indication that he 'might not be such a bad sort' (p. 69) if he is prepared to amuse children. The action between Paul and Lola is taking place after the twins have gone to their bath, and results in Lola's injuries.

GLOSSARY

64	**rowing eight** team of eight men who row a long, narrow boat. Both Oxford and Cambridge Universities have a long tradition of competitive rowing
64	**set** a communal set of rooms at university comprising a sitting room, two bedrooms and a small kitchen, or gyp room
64	**gyp** manservant, or female equivalent, who waited in the gyp room until called
64	**Halls** dining halls
64	**Maids' Dancing** the 'Maid's Party' is a party in Girton at the end of Michaelmas (autumn) term with entertainments and dancing
64	**Little-Go** entrance examination undergraduates had to sit before being allowed to enter the university to study for a degree
65	**'Varsity** university
65	**bluestocking** academic woman; slightly derogatory
65	**High Table** the table at which Fellows (members of the academic staff) sit for dinner. The tables for students are arranged along the Hall; High Table is on a dais, or platform, across the Hall

CHAPTER 7

- In a temper, Briony is on the island swiping the heads off stinging nettles with a stick.
- Her brother drives past in the trap with Paul Marshall but does not stop to talk to her. Disillusioned with attacking nettles, she walks back to the bridge.

The action of the novel has now reverted to the moments before the arrival of Leon and Paul Marshall. Briony has gone to the ruined temple on the island and is venting her frustration by attacking stinging nettles with a peeled hazel switch. She imagines that they represent her cousins and punishes them for spoiling her play. She then turns on playwriting as her victim, and finally the earlier stages of her childhood, in an act of 'self-purification' (p. 74) to make way for her new, older self.

Briony imagines her talent in slashing nettles being recognised and she plays out a fantasy drama of performing at the Olympics. Leon approaches in the trap, but she refuses to acknowledge him. When he passes without stopping, she gets tired of hitting nettles and makes her way towards the house, but is not ready to go in so waits on the bridge for something to happen.

COMMENTARY

Briony's anger has given way to indulgent and enjoyable destruction. She has taken the time to peel a stick before launching an assault on the nettles and finds the activity satisfying. Typically, her imagination takes over and she makes a **narrative** of what she is doing. The depiction of the scene is benign, and we smile at Briony's activity and enjoy it with her rather than laugh at her. The venom with which she assaults nettles representing Lola is disarmed by the childish context.

This activity leads Briony into an even more childish reverie as she imagines herself lauded as a world champion nettle-slasher at the Olympic Games. In conjuring up this picture she adopts the terms of a sports commentator, analysing her movements and technique.

CONTEXT

The temple is the ruin of a neoclassical folly – a building intended largely to decorate the landscape, built in the style of classical Greek or Roman architecture and popular on country estates in the mid and late eighteenth century.

PART ONE CHAPTER 7 continued

CONTEXT

Writing about the impact of quantum physics on the intellectual landscape of the twentieth century, McEwan has said: 'The observer is a part of what he observes. Reality is changed by the presence of the observer – he can no longer pretend to be invisible' (Introduction to *Or Shall We Die?* (Jonathan Cape, 1983), p. 17).

We have the sense of her being watched, or watching herself, and imagining the impact on others or how she would be described. She is disappointed that Leon does not stop the trap and speak to her. Even though she had anticipated having to 'suffer the interruption with good grace' (p. 75), she was secretly hoping he would stop as it would demonstrate interest in her. Her happy picture of her activity deflates and she becomes 'a solitary girl swiping nettles with a stick' (p. 76), robbed of any significance. She is struck by the futility of her activity but also of all she can do; her circumstances are frustratingly limited.

By the end of the chapter, she has lapsed into petulance. She is once again the child demanding to be noticed, hoping to be the centre of someone's universe, but with the growing and annoying recognition that she is not: 'She would simply wait on the bridge, calm and obstinate, until events, real events, not her own fantasies, rose to her challenge, and dispelled her insignificance' (p. 77). Her challenge will be met the same evening by the events that unfold, and Briony's desire to be important will be the catalyst for disaster.

GLOSSARY

72	**Nicholas Revett** English architect (1721–1804). With James Stuart he published *The Antiquities of Athens*, illustrating in detail the relics of classical Greek buildings and encouraging neoclassical architecture in England
72	**laths** strips of wood that formed the studwork over which walls were built
75	**Berlin Olympics** the Olympic Games for 1936 had been awarded to Germany before the Nazis came to power

CHAPTER 8

- Robbie, in his mother's bungalow, reflects on his new feelings for Cecilia.
- He drafts a letter to her and then deliberately spoils his copy by adding an obscene ending.
- On the way to the hall, he finds Briony waiting on the bridge and gives her the letter to take ahead to Cecilia.
- Too late, Robbie realises he has left the good copy of the letter at home and has put into the envelope the obscene copy.

Robbie has returned home and bathed and the chapter opens with him looking at the landscape in the fading evening light. The house is small and cramped, and we feel aware of his bulk crammed into the tiny room in contrast to the open spaces of the garden and the Tallises' house. He runs over in his mind Cecilia's undressing and plunge into the pool, realising that although he has never thought about her as anything other than a childhood companion he is now drawn to her sexually. Realising she must be annoyed that he is coming to dinner, he drafts a letter to her. He makes several attempts before successfully typing a letter that he feels has the right balance of seriousness and levity. Then he spontaneously types an obscene ending to his letter and rips it from the typewriter. He copies the letter out longhand, without the obscenities, and then gets dressed for dinner.

Robbie walks slowly to the Tallis house, contemplating the happy future he envisages as a successful and cultured doctor. It is a sad **irony** that he is so certain of this ideal future but, as we later discover, will not live to enjoy it. He meets Briony on the bridge and asks her to take his letter to Cecilia. When it is too late to stop her, he realises with terrible certainty that he left the hand-written copy of the letter on the anatomy book in his study and has given Briony the obscene version.

CONTEXT

Fauvism (p. 78) was an artistic movement, led by Henri Matisse (1869–1954), which flourished at the turn of the twentieth century. Fauvists used brilliantly coloured paints applied directly from the tube to achieve astonishing boldness and vibrancy. They favoured scenes copied from nature.

CONTEXT

Gray's Anatomy is a definitive text on anatomy by Henry Gray (1825–61), first published in 1858. It has been through many editions since. The illustration referred to as number 1236 was in fact not labelled as such until the 1962 edition. This would have been easy for McEwan to check, so is perhaps one of Briony's errors and evidence of a reworking of the novel in the 1960s.

COMMENTARY

The chapter opens with a new voice, but it is not until the second paragraph that we discover it belongs to Robbie. It is clearly an educated and cultured voice.

Robbie's style is more assured and less literary than Cecilia's – it could be evidence of his greater accomplishment, that gave him a first class degree and her only a third. His voice and **character** are important, as he will relate the second part of the book.

Robbie's reflections on the incident with Cecilia reveal not only to us but also to himself how his feelings about her have changed. Unlike Briony, who waits for something to happen, he takes decisive action in writing to Cecilia. This decisiveness will stand him in good stead during the coming war. After the careful control of phrasing his letter, he lets his real feelings come out in the obscene ending he adds to the typed version. Although Robbie refers to Sigmund Freud a few times in interpreting his own actions, he states that putting the wrong letter into the envelope doesn't need to be analysed in this way. His denial immediately suggests the opposite to us – that this was subconsciously deliberate, to precipitate a crisis with Cecilia which gives him the chance to act and know her feelings.

This chapter is important in revealing Robbie's character and fills in his background to give a fuller view of his personality and how it has developed. In a novel in which the links between events over time is such an important theme, it is not surprising that we see how Robbie's character has been forged from events in his earlier life. His mother was abandoned by his father when Robbie was young. His father's complete disappearance enabled his mother to invent a romantic story for him – running away to the First World War and dying for his country – which is preferable to any of the more likely scenarios. Robbie sees the potential for this desertion even in their wedding photograph – again, future events are given roots in the past.

Robbie gives examples of how he has confounded people's expectations of his class. Though Cecilia thought he removed his shoes to make a point about social status, he says he did it to avoid treading on the floor Polly had just cleaned, and then removed his

CONTEXT

Sigmund Freud (1856–1939) was an influential Austrian neurologist who founded psychology. He explained many traits of character and behaviour as having their roots in suppressed sexual feelings or events in a patient's personal history.

socks in case they were smelly. The implication is that Cecilia is more aware of the class difference, and Robbie doesn't care about it. But he makes too much of a point of denying the importance of class for us to accept that it is of no significance.

GLOSSARY

79	**farthing coin**	worth one quarter of an old penny (1d), measuring 20mm in diameter
82	**Mr Eliot**	the poet T. S. Eliot (1888–1965), who won the Nobel Prize for Literature in 1948. He edited the quarterly review, *Criterion*, from 1922 to 1939, and was known for his generous encouragement of young poets
82	**Malvolio**	character in Shakespeare's play, *Twelfth Night*, who is made a fool by his love of a woman who is not interested in him.
83	**battels**	bill for provisions provided by a college buttery (usually wine and college meals)
84	**Versailles**	Palace of Versailles outside Paris, France. The landscaped gardens, designed by André Le Nôtre (1613–1700), included fountains with water that looked magically still, a triumph of engineering
85	**carbon**	carbon paper – a thin film with powdered carbon on one side which was sandwiched between two sheets of paper to make a copy of a page as it was typed
85	**TB**	tuberculosis – a deadly respiratory disease
87	***Daily Sketch***	popular tabloid newspaper published between 1909 and 1971
88	**Front**	frontline of combat in the First World War; most British men who died in the First World War were killed in the trenches of the battlefields in northern France

CHAPTER 9

- Cecilia talks with Leon on the terrace, but is ill at ease.
- Briony manages to slip Robbie's note to Cecilia.
- Cecilia maintains her composure while reading the note, but realises that Briony must have read it before handing it to her.

? QUESTION

How important is social class in the unfolding of character and events in *Atonement*?

CONTEXT

The influential literary critic F. R. Leavis (1895–1978) (p. 91) taught English at Cambridge from 1925 to 1962. He introduced a new, serious style of literary criticism that required critics to look at the life and moral opinions of the writer. He was a demanding and severe teacher.

CONTEXT

The cubist Spanish painter Pablo Picasso (1881–1973) frequently jumbled up the features of his subjects, combining elements from several different views of a face in a single canvas.

CHECK THE NET

To find out about the works of Pablo Picasso, look at **www.picasso.fr/anglais/**

Cecilia is unsettled, changing her dress twice before she is satisfied with her appearance, which she sees distorted and 'Picasso-like' (p. 99) in her mirror. On the way out of her room the last time, she is surprised by Jackson and is side-tracked into sorting out the twins' problem of having only one pair of socks between them.

In the kitchen, she mediates between her mother and the cook, arguing over Emily's desire to cancel the roast dinner and make salad. Cecilia persuades her mother to offer guests a choice, satisfying both parties. Free at last to drink gin and tonic with her brother on the terrace, Cecilia talks nervously with him, finding it difficult to move beyond their childhood relationship.

Briony avoids her mother's attempt to send her away to clean up and passes Robbie's note to Cecilia. Cecilia takes in the message, including the obscene postscript, without betraying any surprise or shock. But she quickly realises that Robbie would not have sent it as a folded note and that Briony has read it.

COMMENTARY

This chapter reveals more of Cecilia's **character**. She sees herself as essential to managing and soothing the household. She feels obliged to help the twins, she negotiates for the cook, finding a solution that does not undermine or embarrass her mother, and intends also to look for Briony – 'Someone else to worry about' (p. 101). Cecilia detects no **irony** in Leon's comment on her adopting the role of mother as it matches her own view of herself.

Cecilia slips back into her habitual way of relating to Leon and there is little evidence of the sophistication she claims to have developed at Cambridge. She adores him, and sees him as suave, relaxed, carefree – though to us he appears shallow with only superficial interests and a dull life as a banker. She is anxious and unsure, overcompensating by trying to be witty, but is aware that she is not coming across well, and is self-conscious.

After reading Robbie's note, Cecilia quickly recognises her own feelings for Robbie. She deduces that an unacknowledged interest in him has worked subconsciously to keep her near him but made her encounters with him awkward. While this may be true, it is also convenient for her finally to have an excuse to herself for her inertia.

We see more of Emily, too. The controlling presence that she had imagined for herself is clearly undermined as we see the cook has no respect for her authority. When Cecilia offers a diplomatic solution, Emily complies swiftly, glad to be rid of the difficult task of managing the servants. She sets off to find Briony, but is ineffectual even in this as Briony reappears on her own. She has no impact on Briony, either, in her attempt to send her upstairs to change and ends, instead, smiling indulgently as Briony disregards her.

GLOSSARY

96 **crêpe de Chine** thin silk with a crinkled surface

96 **triptych** arrangement of three pictures, commonly used for religious paintings

97 **flapper dresses** shapeless dresses popular in the 1920s that hang straight from the shoulders to the knees

98 **Shirley Temple** American child film star born 1928. Her first major film was *Little Miss Marker* in 1934

102 **neo-Gothic** fake Gothic (medieval) style popular in the eighteenth and nineteenth centuries. In buildings, it is characterised by flying buttresses and vaulting arches

104 **Gloucester Old Spot** breed of pig

104 **nacreous** having the appearance of mother-of-pearl

108 **stroke** oarsman who sits nearest to the stern and sets the pace for the other rowers

108 *Private Lives* society comedy by Noël Coward (1899–1973), first performed in 1930

108 **Gilbert and Sullivan** comic opera by the English librettist William Schwenck Gilbert (1836–1911) and Sir Arthur Seymour Sullivan (1842–1900)

108 **Albany** residential hotel in central London

109 *Paradise Lost* epic poem in ten books by John Milton (1608–74) relating the biblical history of man's fall from grace

CONTEXT

One of the most complete examples of neo-Gothic architecture is Strawberry Hill, the house of eccentric parliamentarian Horace Walpole who wrote one of the first Gothic novels in the English language, *The Castle of Otranto* (1764).

Chapter 10

- Briony is in her room when Lola comes in and shows her scratches and Chinese burns that she says the twins have inflicted on her.
- Briony sympathises and tells her about the letter, pleased with the shocked reaction it elicits from Lola.
- On the way down to dinner, Briony disturbs Robbie and Cecilia making love in the darkened library. She thinks Robbie is attacking Cecilia.

CHECK THE BOOK

A good introduction to McEwan's own approach to writing is David Malcolm's *Understanding Ian McEwan* (2002).

Briony mulls over the obscene word in the letter, relishing her feeling of disgust. She wonders how to write about what has happened and the new, adult insight into life she considers it has given her. She drifts into a meditation on writing and what it requires, reflecting that she can describe things well but needs to learn how to capture and show emotions.

When Lola comes in and shows her injuries, Briony feels the grown-up responsibility to console her. In an attempt to look mature herself, and to have a dramatic secret of her own to share, she tells Lola about Robbie's letter. She is gratified by Lola's evident shock and the two encourage each other in working up Robbie as a threat and a 'maniac' (p. 119), a word that Briony finds very appealing.

On the way down to dinner, Briony goes to the library where she makes out two figures in the dark. At first she wonders if she imagines them, but then recognises Cecilia and Robbie. She misinterprets their stance and thinks Robbie is attacking Cecilia. She stares in shock, not knowing what to do, until Cecilia eventually straightens her clothes and walks past Briony, out of the room. Briony follows her sister, certain that she has rescued her from a dangerous assault.

Commentary

By the end of this chapter, the misconceptions that will spiral irrevocably to the crisis of the novel are in place and the action takes on a fatal inevitability from this point.

The chapter is important in developing Briony's **character** as well as the action. Her image of herself as a writer is very much in the foreground, and the theme of writing is explored further through this. As Briony plays with the obscene word Robbie has used, not everything passing through her mind is convincing for a child of thirteen. She deduces the meaning of the word from a context that is distinctly adult, and demonstrates anatomical knowledge that is not consistent with her claim that not even her mother had ever mentioned that part of the body. We might feel that the voice of the older Briony breaks through the **narrative** here. Further, Briony comments that she is quite able to capture the reality of things in description, but struggles to convey emotion rather than state it: 'how was [sadness] itself put across so it could be felt in all its lowering immediacy?' (p. 116). This is a common theme of creative writing courses and seems to belong more to the later writer than to the thirteen-year-old Briony.

Again, Briony feels that she is leaving childhood behind and is being initiated into an adult world of mysteries that she can't quite grasp but must come to terms with if she is to write successfully. She decides she must reject the simple, clear morality familiar to her from children's books. However, this is precisely what she returns to in damning Robbie and reconsidering her previous encounters with him in the light of what she thinks she has discovered. She and Lola indulge in a childish frenzy of over-dramatising events and working Robbie up as a terrible and dangerous villain. It is in this over-wrought state, with her imagination running away with her, that she comes across the lovers in the library and sees what she expects to see – an unwelcome assault rather than a shared moment of passion.

Briony's desire for drama in her life, which has been clear from the start of the book, makes her fix eagerly on the supposed threat of Robbie. What could have been comical as a juvenile misunderstanding of adult passion is dangerously distorted by her desire for drama, sensation and attention. By chance, it becomes the catalyst for disaster.

> **CONTEXT**
>
> 'There was an old lady who swallowed a fly' (p. 115) is a line from a comic song. An old lady swallows a fly, then a spider to eat it, then a bird to eat the spider, and so on until she dies after eating a horse. The parallel is clear – a simple, harmless occurrence sets in motion a train of events that snowballs, ending in catastrophe because of an inappropriate reaction.

> **GLOSSARY**
>
> 114 **Cam by Grantchester meadow** the River Cam which runs through Cambridge; students frequently punt from Cambridge to the nearby village of Grantchester, often stopping at the meadow to picnic
>
> 117 **lariat** lasso or rope for tethering animals

CHAPTER 11

- Dinner is awkward, marred by aggressive remarks and suppressed feelings.
- Robbie recalls events since his arrival at the house: explaining his mistake to Cecilia, making love in the library, and being interrupted by Briony.
- The twins leave the table and Briony reveals the scratches and bruises they have supposedly inflicted on Lola.
- Briony discovers a note the twins have left, saying they are running away. The party breaks up as all, except Emily, set out to search for the boys.

? QUESTION
Look at the language McEwan uses on p. 125 to build up the atmosphere of stifled tension. What effect does it have on your involvement as a reader?

The diners are uncommunicative, stifled by the heat, the cloying chocolate cocktails and the unwelcome prospect of a roast dinner. There is a lot of suppressed emotion – Robbie and Cecilia are preoccupied by their interrupted love-making, and Briony by the threat she thinks Robbie poses to her sister. Emily's inability to make the social situation run smoothly means that it gets off to a slow start.

Robbie drifts into recalling in detail what happened in the library with Cecilia and this flashback fills in the **narrative** for us. The dinner degenerates into bickering and sniping as Briony is tetchy and Cecilia vindictive.

When the twins leave the table, the tense, difficult atmosphere is broken first by the revelation of Lola's injuries. When Briony finds the twins' note, the group breaks up to search for them. Robbie, confident that the twins cannot have got far, is annoyed at feeling cheated of his planned tryst with Cecilia in the dark gardens. Displeased that Leon insists Cecilia goes with him, Robbie decides to search on his own.

COMMENTARY

The atmosphere in the dining room is stifling – both from the physical heat and the emotions held in check. Paul's sickly cocktail, the inappropriate warm dessert and the obligation to eat too much contribute to the suffocating fullness of the scene. In the room, as in the food and drinks, excess and extravagance are cloying and irritating. This mirrors the way the novel is building up. There has been a run of small incidents, blown out of proportion by the characters but with an impact that has been contained, giving a sense of building pressure. Some cool, fresh relief is needed to counteract the heat of the evening, the over-rich food, the suppressed passions and the stodgily ornate house. The flashback to Cecilia and Robbie's love-making in the library, and the spatting at the table, build the pressure further.

While the diners eat, Robbie recollects the interval in the library with Cecilia. He recalls very precisely, with evocative description, exactly how he felt, what her body was like and what they did. The level of detail is surprising, even shocking, in its intimacy. The episode of passion is given extended treatment as it is to be the only one they can enjoy, and memories of it must sustain both the lovers through Robbie's imprisonment and the war. We need this level of detail in order to understand what it is that Robbie recreates in Part Two of the novel.

Lola's injuries, revealed to the table by Briony, are still presented as though inflicted by the twins. There are clues for us that this is not true. At the time when Lola claimed the twins attacked her, we saw her letting them into the room and talking to them. They told Cecilia they were afraid to ask Lola to help them find socks, and it seemed 'wondrous' (p. 118) to Briony that the twins could have upset Lola so much. Paul, who is also scratched, says that he had to pull the twins off Lola – yet we saw the whole of his encounter with Lola and the twins and it did not happen.

CONTEXT

The line 'nothing that can be … hopes' (p. 131) is a quotation from Shakespeare's *Twelfth Night*, III.4.81–2. Malvolio says this when anticipating consummation of his desire for Olivia, but he is thwarted. The use of this quotation in Robbie's thoughts here tells us that although the consummation of their desire looks inevitable, things can (and will) still go wrong. There are several references and allusions to *Twelfth Night* in *Atonement*.

CHECK THE BOOK

Lady Chatterley's Lover, which Robbie thinks of on p. 132, was written in 1928 by D. H. Lawrence (1885–1930). It relates a passionate affair between the wife of a disabled aristocrat and her gamekeeper, Mellors. The erotic detail was so shocking at the time the book was written that it was banned in the UK until 1960. It was privately printed in Florence, Italy, by the bookseller Giuseppe Orioli. Pirated editions appeared on the black market immediately.

The disappearance of the twins, which elicits annoyance from Robbie, sets the crisis of the novel in motion. Robbie's frustration leads him to go out into the night to search alone for them. In another glimpse forward, we are told that he would reflect many times that this seemingly slight choice 'transformed his life' (p. 144).

GLOSSARY

126 **grace** short prayer of thanks spoken before food

128 **Spode** china or porcelain made by the English potter Joshua Spode (1754–1827) or his company

128 **Barsac** sweet, white, French Sauternes wine usually drunk with dessert, but occasionally with a first course; it would not go with roast meat. 1921 was a good year for Barsac and the wine would have been expensive

128 **Charlotte Street** street in the Bloomsbury area of central London

138 **tantric art** tantric sex involves keeping still to delay or avoid the moment of climax to enjoy instead spiritual union, and to channel energies. Tantrism is a movement within Hinduism

CHAPTER 12

- Emily Tallis has remained in the house. She is certain the twins will return and does not call the police.

- When her husband telephones, he is displeased that she has not called the police and intends to do so himself.

- The conversation between Emily and her husband is interrupted by the arrival of Cecilia, Leon, Briony and Lola, in distress. Leon speaks to his father but will not immediately tell Emily what has happened.

Through most of the chapter, Emily is sitting in the house waiting for her husband to call and the twins to be found. She does not think the twins are in any danger and reflects resentfully on how Lola seems to want to be the centre of attention, as her own sister, Lola's mother, did.

Her thoughts turn to her husband. He is clearly having an affair, but she does not want to confront him. She is content to wait until, in old age, he returns to her. She considers the war preparation work he is doing at the ministry to be 'silly' (p. 150) and an exaggeration of the threat.

She again mourns the imminent end of Briony's childhood and her own acceleration towards old age and death, then reflects on her husband's patronage of Robbie, which she considers inappropriate and unnecessary. Finally, she wonders whether Paul Marshall would make a good husband for Cecilia.

When her husband telephones, Emily relates domestic trivia to him before revealing the twins' disappearance. Jack realises the seriousness of the situation and tells her he will call the police. At that moment, Leon, Cecilia, Briony and Lola come in, and Lola's expression tells Emily that something terrible has happened. Leon speaks to his father on the phone and then leads Emily into another room to tell her the news.

COMMENTARY

The chapter is important in revealing more about Emily and the dysfunctional nature of the Tallis family. Emily decides not to phone the police, partly because she does not like the policeman or his wife, but mostly because she believes (or wants to believe) that the twins will return unharmed in a short time. She is almost incapable of action of any kind. As her musings wander between topics she reveals that she will not confront her husband about the affair she knows he is having, and we have already seen her fail to have any effect on the household. Her inertia extends to what she expects of others and how she views their behaviour. She believes preparations for a possible war are over-dramatising the risk, that Jack should not interfere in Robbie's life by paying for his education, and even that Robbie's plans for the garden are pointless as she will be dead before the plants have grown to an appreciable size. She sees her own life as having its focus in Briony, and as the girl grows up Emily is on a downhill path to the grave. Her life has after all turned out to be 'massive and empty' (p. 151) as she has wasted it on superficialities.

> **CONTEXT**
>
> By 1935, most people thought that war in Europe was inevitable. Emily's refusal to think about the threat or take seriously the projections of casualties is characteristic of her.

QUESTION
By encouraging us as well as Emily to jump to a false conclusion – that the twins are dead – Briony/McEwan draws us into the same pattern of error as will soon precipitate the calamity. What effect does our false assumption have on our ability to judge Briony harshly for 'knowing' something that is not true?

CONTEXT
The phrase 'Ploughshares into tinfoil' (p. 153) comes from a verse in the Bible: 'Beat your plowshares into swords, and your pruning hooks into spears', Joel 3:10. Jack Tallis is being dismissive of Paul Marshall's ambition here, suggesting he is using valuable resources to make something useless. A ploughshare is the blade of a plough that cuts through the earth.

Emily resents the twins and Lola as reminders of her sister, who was always the centre of attention as a child. This gives another reason for her reluctance to call the police. However, when Jack Tallis phones she tells him a host of other details before mentioning the loss of the twins. His question 'And where were they after all?' (p. 154) shows that he assumes, because of the way she has told him the story, that they have already been found. This throws her lack of concern into sharp relief. When Leon talks to his father on the phone, events are removed from the control of the ineffectual Emily at last.

It is still not clear at the end of this chapter that Lola has been assaulted. The assumption which we and Emily are bound to make is that the twins have been found dead. Even so, Emily is so self-centred as to assume that Leon is concerned about her falling in shock and hurting herself. She does not want to hear what he is telling Jack on the phone, being anxious to remain excluded from any action for as long as possible.

GLOSSARY

150	**shot silk** silk woven so that the colour seems to change when the fabric moves; achieved by weaving warp and weft (horizontal and vertical threads) from different colours
151	**ceonothus** hardy shrub with blue or lilac flowers (California lilac)
151	**pergola** decorative trellis framework in a garden over which plants are trained
151	**wisteria** slow-growing, woody, climbing plant with long, hanging clusters of flowers, usually purple
151	**reefers** cigarettes made with cannabis. The possession of cannabis became illegal in the UK in 1928

CHAPTER 13

- Going to the island to look for the twins, Briony discovers Lola on the ground with a man, who leaves as she approaches.
- Lola says very little, but Briony decides she has been attacked by Robbie.
- Briony helps Lola towards the house, then Cecilia and Leon appear and Leon carries Lola back.

Here the **narrative** moves back in time again to Briony's search for the twins. She goes through the motions of looking for the twins but is confident they will be safe. She enjoys the chance to practise describing the episode in her writing, imagining the twins floating face down in the pool, and reflects again on how she is crossing the border into adulthood. She revels in Robbie's hatred and imagines what else might be happening in the darkness and how her own future might unfold. At one point she hears a shout in the distance and sees a torch flash on and off – later we might wonder if this was perhaps part of the incident between Paul and Lola, or just an innocent part of the search.

Briony sees her mother lying on the couch inside and spies on her briefly. Emily looks old and tired, leading Briony to imagine her funeral. She considers going in, but decides instead to head off to the island. A few times on the way she almost turns back, as it is so dark, but in the end she presses ahead. She hears a cry from the bridge, which at first she imagines is a startled duck, and only later realises was human. She is strangely unperturbed by the apparent movement of the bush for which she mistakes Lola and Paul, who are lying on the grass on the way to the temple. When she disturbs them, Lola speaks and the other figure walks away. Much is made of how little Briony can make out in the darkness. It is clearly absurd that Briony can claim to know the identity of the man when she was at first certain he was a bush. All this is set to undermine Briony's later certainty.

As Briony soothes Lola, she suggests explanations to her – Lola says very little herself. Briony convinces herself that Lola has been attacked by Robbie and persuades Lola that she saw him. Pleased to adopt the role of mature helper, Briony launches enthusiastically into the task of comforting Lola and helping her to the house, until Leon and Cecilia meet them and Leon carries Lola back.

COMMENTARY

The flow of time is tangled by this chapter which is itself set earlier than the end of the previous chapter. It opens with a leap into the future, referring to Briony's crime yet to be committed. This piques our interest – we have now heard so much about an ensuing disaster

> **CONTEXT**
>
> While Briony only imagines her mother's death, in *The Cement Garden* (1978), two orphans hide their mother's body in the cellar. There is no suggestion Briony wants her mother dead; she is more interested in the attention she would receive at the funeral. There is, however, a morbid feel to Briony's projection reminiscent of McEwan's earlier writing.

that we are keen to find out what it is and welcome this reassurance that it will be revealed soon. It continues a pattern already established in the **narrative** of moving backwards and forwards through time to manipulate our expectations and responses.

Briony is preoccupied with her own concerns – with how she feels she is growing up, and how she can turn experiences into literature. Her fertile imagination builds potential narratives and possible futures from any scrap of event or fleeting thought. These fantasies combine her desire for excitement, her literary ambitions (she ponders how she will write about them) and her need for attention. In considering her mother's funeral she stresses that 'It had to be witnessed' (p. 162). This is the same desire to see others seeing her that Cecilia has exhibited earlier.

CHECK THE BOOK

McEwan shows a catastrophe precipitated by a seemingly insignificant act or decision in many of his works. In *The Child in Time* (1987), a father's moment of inattention leads to his daughter's permanent disappearance.

As Briony draws towards the island and her discovery of Lola, there are many overt reminders that events could have gone differently – that she might have turned back, that she could have stayed in the room with her mother – and then the crisis would have been averted. The slightest reasons impel events in the particular direction they finally take – Robbie's decision to search alone, Briony's reluctance to explain why she was looking through the window, her unwillingness to give in to fear, and her desire to appear grown up.

On pages 167–71, in the space between the repetition of the words 'I can. And I will', the inevitability of all that follows is spelt out. The certainty in those words, though ill-founded, seals the fate of all the characters involved. We see forward to the future weeks during which Briony sticks to her story and Lola remains silent. The blameworthiness of Briony in particular, but also of Lola, is held up to scrutiny – Briony was only a child, she was not helped to re-examine her story, but felt only encouragement to stick with it. She would feel the disapproval of adults if she faltered in her certainty and, for a child like Briony, desperate for adult attention and to feel important, this was certain to make her ignore any doubts and follow the path mapped out for her.

This chapter is remarkable for the great emphasis it places on description and the visual, especially as it takes place in the dark. We end the chapter with a clear sense that we have seen exactly what has been going on – recreating in us the same error that Briony commits of trusting what we have imagined as a representation of the truth. Even elements of the description which stress how little is visible have their own visual precision: 'the dark disc of Lola's face showed nothing at all' (p. 167).

QUESTION
How culpable is Lola in the tragic events that take place in the novel?

CHAPTER 14

- Lola is taken upstairs and Briony tells her version of events to a policeman.
- Briony retrieves Robbie's note from Cecilia's room and everyone reads it.
- Briony gives her first formal interview to the police, insisting that she saw Robbie on the island.
- In the early morning, Robbie appears with the twins.
- Robbie is arrested.

As Lola is led upstairs sobbing, the police arrive. Briony relates her version of events, saying that she saw Robbie. The family doctor arrives to examine Lola. Downstairs, everyone but Cecilia talks in small groups; Cecilia is angry and upset, and stands apart smoking.

Remembering Robbie's note, Briony rushes to find it, then gives it to the policeman. Cecilia is furious when she discovers that everyone has read it and storms off to her room.

Briony gives her first official statement. She shows the positions in which she saw Robbie and Cecilia in the library, and insists again that she definitely saw Robbie on the island.

In the early morning, Robbie appears through the morning mist carrying one of the twins on his shoulders and accompanied by the other. Briony is sent indoors before he arrives at the house. She is incensed that he may be hailed as a hero and her own actions forgotten.

From her room, Briony sees Robbie taken away, handcuffed, in the police car. Still firm in her belief that she understands all she sees, Briony interprets Cecilia's last exchange with Robbie as generous forgiveness. As the car drives away Robbie's mother, Grace, appears on the drive to stand in front of it. She launches an assault, screaming that they are all liars, and hitting the car with an umbrella. Robbie is driven away.

COMMENTARY

The chapter opens with a glimpse of the future, showing how Briony will later be tortured by remorse as a result of what happened in the immediate aftermath of the attack. It is the night of the attack and the early morning that followed that will trouble her more than the legal processes that will unfold in the subsequent weeks. The rest of the chapter sets out how this future situation will come about.

For the first time in the novel, a lot of real action takes place – Briony's desire for excitement has been fulfilled. She revels in being centre stage.

The chapter is sprinkled with doubt about the older Briony's memories of events. She questions how she can remember seeing the doctor arrive when she knows that she must have been in another room with her mother, for instance. The doubt of the older Briony casts the certainty of her former self into relief.

Briony tries hard to convince herself, as well as the police and her family, of what she saw. Her motive for doing this is not malice against Robbie, but a desire for a neat story, to see things work out as she feels they should to create a **narrative** with integrity. She does not pause, at this age, to reflect that life is not a balanced narrative and in trying to impose one she wrecks the lives of the people she uses as **characters**.

It is partly to bolster her own certainty that Briony rushes to find Robbie's letter. **Ironically**, handing over the letter gives her a feeling of doing good, yet a motivating factor is 'that [it] could only earn

CONTEXT

Psychological studies have shown that people may often build false memories. The psychologist Jean Piaget (1896–1980) described an example of this, explaining how our minds may store accounts we hear of events but later recall them as though they were real memories. Briony has previously said (p. 41) that she thinks she recalls her own retelling of events rather than original experience.

her praise' (p. 177). Her desire to remain the star of the scene is strongly underlined by her private fury that Robbie should turn up with the twins. She fears that he will be lauded as a hero and that she will be overshadowed.

At one key point in the investigation, Briony is given a clear chance to escape from the action she has set in motion. She tells the policeman 'I know it was him', and the policeman replies 'Let's forget what you know' (p. 181). At this point, she goes on to confirm repeatedly that she is certain that she saw Robbie, even though this is not true. It is for this, and her later maintenance of this position, that she must spend the rest of the book atoning.

Grace's outburst, heart-wrenching to us as we know she is right and Robbie is innocent, is related dispassionately but fluently by Briony. She does not allow herself to consider Grace's agony – she so far has no capacity to imagine herself in someone else's position. Our own response, though, is of immense sympathy for Grace and a sudden, devastating recognition of the distance between the drama as Briony is seeing it and the terrible reality for Robbie and Grace. The result is a more poignant rendering of the moment than would have been achieved by any expression of sympathy from Briony, the narrator.

> **? QUESTION**
> How does the language of the policeman suggest his occupation and his class?

GLOSSARY

173 **rosary** string of 55 or 165 beads used by Catholics to count a sequence of prayers called 'Aves' as they are recited. Recital of these prayer cycles is often set as a penance for people who have confessed to committing a sin

173 **Humber** type of car commonly used by the British Police in the 1930s

174 **Gladstone bag** leather bag with two equal-sized hinged compartments, commonly used by doctors in the early twentieth century as it could hold a lot of medical equipment

PART TWO

PAGES 191–201

- Robbie Turner is making his way through the French countryside towards Dunkirk accompanied by two corporals, Nettle and Mace.
- He is distressed to see a child's leg stuck in a tree at the site of an air raid.
- At a farmhouse, they are met by a hostile elderly woman and shelter in a barn. Her two sons later bring them good food and drink and they all talk.

The narrative has switched to the perspective of Robbie Turner, now a soldier in war-torn France, and has moved on by five years to 1940. Robbie has been injured in the side but has not told his companions, Nettle and Mace, about his injury. Fever and pain make him absent-minded. Following a shortcut he has identified on the map, they come across a bombed house and Robbie sees a child's severed leg in a tree. He has to go behind a wall to be sick. The soldiers continue on their way, Nettle and Mace teasing Robbie benignly about women. They pass through a swarm of bees, and Robbie's knowledge of rural life saves them from injury.

CHECK THE BOOK

Pillar of Fire: Dunkirk 1940 (2001) by Ronald Atkin, gives a very good account of the Dunkirk evacuation.

They come across a farmhouse and ignore the protests of an elderly woman who tries to drive them away. She claims that her sons will kill the soldiers, but Robbie demands that they have food and water and shelter in a barn. She gives them a scant supply of poor food. Later in the evening, the woman's sons come to the barn. Robbie, Nettle and Mace assume they have come to kill them, and Robbie pulls out his gun, but the men are carrying baguettes, not weapons, and have brought good food and wine. All the men talk, Robbie acting as interpreter. The French brothers tell a sad tale of going to look for a cousin and her children in a bombed-out village, of finding corpses on the road, and of fearing the arrival of the Germany army.

COMMENTARY

The contrast with the first part of the novel is stark. It is not clear for two pages that we are now sharing Robbie's point of view. His style is not instantly recognisable as he has changed in the years that have passed since the action of Part One. In this way he is introduced anew, as though a different **character**.

The spectacle of the child's leg in the tree is shocking, to Robbie and to us. The flat, unemotional account of its fact lets the horror speak for itself. The description of the plane tree first, and then the leg, makes it clear this is a common scene in the war-torn landscape. The fact that Robbie is embarrassed by his disgust and his subsequent need to vomit is testament to how many horrors the men have witnessed – the others are able to disregard it and Robbie fears they will see it as weakness that he cannot. This leg is the 'unexpected detail' (p. 191) referred to at the start of the chapter, and stays with Robbie as a disturbing image that he struggles to get out of his mind.

The hostility of the old woman is initially comic, though dangerous in that it nearly leads to her sons later being shot by Robbie. We reflect differently on her behaviour on hearing that she had already lost a son in the First World War and that she has become confused by old age and grief. The brothers' account of their journey, and their disappointment and wonder that the German army is again in France, make real the human impact of the war.

CHECK THE FILM
Artistic depictions of the Second World War have often idealised or glorified it. The opening scene of the film *Saving Private Ryan* (1998), about the D-Day landings in 1944, presents a stark picture of the horrors of war similar to that of *Atonement*. It is set in the same area of northern France.

CONTEXT
Most French and British casualties in the First World War were in the battlefields of northern France. Opposing armies dug themselves into trenches and launched infantry assaults on the enemy, the armies moving only a few yards at a time and both sides sustaining horrific losses. Over 3 million British and 6 million French soldiers were killed or wounded. This was three-quarters of the French troops.

GLOSSARY

191	**West Kents** the Royal West Kents, a regiment of the British army; five battalions of the West Kents fought in northern France in 1940
191	**the last time** the First World War, also fought on the fields of northern France
193	**basic training** gruelling preparatory training undertaken by soldiers
195	**'C'est impossible … rester ici'** 'It is impossible, sir. You can't stay here.'
196	**RASC** Royal Army Service Corps – catering division of the British army
196	**Heal's in the Tottenham Court Road** furniture store north of Oxford Street in London

CONTEXT

Short for *Sturzkampfflugzeug* – 'dive-bomber' in German – a 'Stuka' (p. 200) was a single-engine monoplane widely used by the German airforce during the first half of the Second World War. It dropped its bombs while still diving towards the ground, pulling up after the bombs had been released. It could carry one very large bomb (1,000 lbs), or one large and two small bombs.

GLOSSARY CONTINUED

197 **Fifth columnists** a term dating from the Spanish Civil War (1936–9) but used generally for subversive agents who have infiltrated an enemy population or political structure; in this case, men who sympathise with the Nazi cause but are disguised within the French population

197 **Mosley** Sir Oswald Mosley, 6th baronet (1896–1980); British politician, fascist sympathiser of Adolf Hitler and leader of the British Union of Fascists

197 **Lee-Enfields** short, magazine-loaded rifles used by the British infantry during the Second World War

197 **'Bonsoir, Messieurs'** 'Good evening, gentlemen'

198 **'Anglais? Belges?'** 'English? Belgian?'

198 **'Vive l'Angleterre'** 'Long live England'

198 **Arras** town in northern France, capital of the Pas-de-Calais *département*

200 **sappers blowing a bridge in the retreat** Royal Engineers using explosives to blow up bridges as the British army withdrew towards Dunkirk. They did this to make it more difficult for the German army to follow them

200 **Verdun in 1915** French town of Verdun, on the front line for three years during the First World War

PAGES 202–13

- Robbie cannot sleep and leaves the barn.
- He reflects on his only meeting with Cecilia after leaving prison and being sent to France.
- He reads through Cecilia's last letter, which offers some hope that Briony may at last admit that she was wrong.

Unable to sleep, Robbie feels the wound in his side, which is throbbing uncomfortably, confirming his suspicion that it has a piece of shrapnel in it. He reflects sadly on the boy killed in his bed, on the thoughtlessness of the bombers, and then on his own lost youth wasted in prison. He gets up and watches the flashes in the sky from distant gunfire and thinks about the possibility of being captured and spending the rest of the war in a prison camp, knowing he would not survive a second incarceration.

Robbie goes back to bed but continues recalling the past, thinking about his last meeting with Cecilia and how her letters sustained him in prison. The two had become intimate in their letters, writing in code and referring to books they knew in order to bypass the censorship of the prison wardens. Their meeting for tea in London was awkward, but they shared a long kiss before Cecilia took her bus back to the hospital. Their plans to meet before Robbie was sent to France were thwarted by the early declaration of war.

He reads a letter from Cecilia in which she tells him of Briony's wish to meet up and Cecilia's hope that it might mean Briony wants to set the record straight and clear Robbie's name.

COMMENTARY

The combination of his earlier life and his time in prison have prepared Robbie well for the army and France, and explain the regard in which Nettle and Mace hold him, despite his inferior rank (Robbie could not apply to be an officer because of his criminal record). His accounts of the stifling oppression of prison, compared with which the routine in the army seems liberating, make the consequences of Briony's actions painfully real.

Cecilia's final letter is given in its entirety, so that her voice can convey her love for him and her reaction to Briony's change of mind. It gives us a chance to see how she has changed. She has grown up, and learnt to deal with trauma – the daily agonies she witnesses as a nurse as well as her years spent waiting for Robbie and her rejection of her family have moulded her adult **character**. It also gives the first clue of how she views Briony. In her first letter to Robbie on the subject, Cecilia makes clear that she will never forgive the rest of her family, but Briony she just does not want to speak to, recognising that her sister was very young and given no chance to change her mind. In the final letter she admits her excitement at the news of Briony's possible retraction and displays a lot of empathy for her sister and her choice to become a nurse. The chapter introduces Briony's atonement, a theme which will occupy the second half of the novel as her crime occupied the first.

> **CONTEXT**
>
> On p. 204, Robbie gives a list of figures from literature to which he compares himself and Cecilia. All are couples for whom love does not go smoothly. Only Emma and George Knightley, from Jane Austen's *Emma* (1816), are happily united at the end of their story.

 CHECK THE BOOK

Alfred Edward Housman (1859–1936) (p. 213) wrote *A Shropshire Lad*, a collection of poems about love and nature, painting an idealised picture of the English countryside. Robbie mentions Housman several times.

CHECK THE BOOK

The lines *'In the nightmare of the dark, All the dogs of Europe bark'* on p. 203 are from the poem 'In Memory of W. B. Yeats', by W. H. Auden. The Irish poet and dramatist W. B. Yeats died in 1939; the lines refer to the hostilities and preparations for war all around Europe.

CHECK THE NET

Information about Lyons teashops, including a menu from 1940, can be found at **www.kzwp.com**

GLOSSARY

203 **raptors** birds of prey

204 **Aldershot** town in Hampshire where regular soldiers in the British army train for combat (and where Ian McEwan was born)

204 **Joe Lyons** a chain of teashops owned by Joe Lyons with branches in London and the provinces in the 1930s and 1940s. They were popular meeting places that offered cheap food and drinks, with a bakery shop at the front

204 **patient Griselde** character in a traditional tale. Her aristocratic husband subjects her to many terrible tests, all of which she bears with fortitude. Eventually he reveals that he was testing her virtue and they live happily

205 **catechism** instruction through a series of questions and responses, particularly in Christian doctrine

207 **Parliament Square** the square in Westminster, London, where the Houses of Parliament and Westminster Abbey stand

207 **'bull'** army slang for drill and equipment-cleaning

207 **been inside** been in prison

210 **Liverpool** a city in northern England, 200 miles from London

210 **Cherbourg** town on the Normandy coast in northern France, north of the city of Caen

210 **British Expeditionary Force** group of one cavalry and six infantry divisions of the British army, formed to fulfil Britain's treaty obligations to help defend France. The BEF was sent to France in 1939 but brought back to Britain when France fell to Germany in 1940

213 **Byron** the **Romantic poet** Lord George Gordon Byron, 6th Baron (1788–1824); he was famous as a lover, had a deformed foot, and died young

213 **Balham** area of south-west London

213 **latrines** lavatories

213 **London Mercury** literary magazine based in London; it was last published in 1939

- Mace and Nettle wake Robbie and they set off again, passing a bombed field littered with fragments of dead cattle.
- They join a long line of retreating British army vehicles, foot soldiers and civilians. When the line is raked by gunfire from a German plane, they take cover.
- Robbie helps an ambulance man with the wounded, Mace and Nettle bury a civilian boy, and they walk on.

After only forty-five minutes sleep, Robbie is woken by the corporals and they set off again across the fields. Robbie, using the map-reading and orienteering skills that he developed in his youth, guides them. His companions' teasing irritates him, and he wants to be rid of them.

Finally, they join a long line of vehicles, soldiers and civilians slowly retreating. Robbie hopes to lose the corporals amongst them, but when he becomes impatient with a civilian driver Mace and Nettle come to his rescue, preventing him hitting the man.

They pass a field in which a cavalry division is shooting their horses, a depressing sight which stalls an argument brewing between Nettle and a couple of Scots infantrymen. Robbie's injury is becoming inflamed and walking is difficult.

A major tries to pull Robbie from the line to join a futile attempt to attack some Germans he says are hiding in the woods, but Robbie is saved by a surprise attack on the column by a German plane. After the attack, Robbie helps move the wounded, and Mace and Nettle help to bury a boy before they continue on their way to Dunkirk.

COMMENTARY

The chapter evokes the weary, slow progress that the men make across the French landscape, the pace of the **narrative** echoing their trudging. They are stalled by the assault from the air, delayed by the major's attempt to recruit them to his ludicrous plan and held up further by their acts of kindness – helping the wounded, giving their

CONTEXT

In retreat, the British army shot their horses and destroyed vehicles that they could not take back to Britain in order to prevent the German army using them. Horses could not be evacuated by boat, nor left to wander the French countryside.

last sips of water to an elderly woman, and burying the boy. We applaud their compassion and generosity, surprising and humbling after all that they have suffered. The nobility of their selfless actions is underlined by Robbie's determination to continue and the narrowing of his focus to just 'walking across the land until he came to the sea' (p. 219). The beat of the words echoes his footfall, and we feel every step of the long, terrible journey.

McEwan is careful to evoke the full horror of the war, here and later in the novel. The young boy they bury had a real life, demonstrated by the row of fountain pens in his pocket. He had a family and social context, represented by the distraught grandparents. Robbie's suppressed distress at seeing the bodies of the women and children in a ditch makes us aware of the relentless barrage of horror he must face, and how he must still focus on his own survival.

There is a touch of humour, even amongst the terrible sights of war. When Robbie glimpses Mace's head on the grass we, like him, fear it is no longer connected to Mace's body. There is macabre comic relief in realising he is only hidden, digging a grave. But the relief is brief, as attention turns to the dead boy who will occupy the grave.

CHECK THE NET

The terrible experience of war in northern France was captured by the war poets of the First World War. Go to the official website of the War Poets Association – **www.warpoets.org** – for more information on poets Siegfried Sassoon, Wilfred Owen, or Rupert Brook.

GLOSSARY

214	**bowie knife** stout hunting knife with a short handle and a guard for the hand
214	**Heinkels** the Heinkel III was the principal bomber plane of the German airforce at the beginning of the Second World War
214	**Luftwaffe** German airforce
215	**Bergues-Furnes canal** canal that runs behind Dunkirk; the need to cross it slowed the retreating army's entry into Dunkirk
215	**ack-ack** the noise of machine gun fire
215	**half-track** army personnel carrier. It has wheels at the front and a caterpillar track at the rear
216	**Bren-gun** air-cooled, gas-operated light machine gun that was one of the principal weapons of the British army in the Second World War. It was renowned as the best light machine gun in the world

GLOSSARY CONTINUED

216   **Panzer division** brigade of tanks and other armoured vehicles used by the German army

217   **Highland Light Infantry** regiment of foot soldiers drawn principally from Glasgow in Scotland

217   **Lille** town in northern France, between Calais and Paris

218   **culvert** covered ditch or channel

218   **HLI** Highland Light Infantry

218   **'It's a braw ... nicht'** 'It's a beautiful, bright moonlight night, tonight'. It is a tradition that only a true Scotsman can pronounce this line properly – hence Nettle's attempt in his Cockney accent annoys the Scotsmen

218   **Cockney** accent or dialect of Londoners, traditionally those born within the area in which the bells of St-Mary-le-Bow church can be heard

219   **A hexameter. Five iambs and an anapaest** a hexameter is a line of verse with six metrical feet; an iamb is a metrical foot with a short syllable followed by a long one; an anapaest has three syllables, two short followed by one long

220   **twenty-five-pounder** a gun that shoots a projectile weighing twenty-five pounds

220   **Buffs Royal East Kent** regiment of the British army

220   **Jerry** slang term for German soldiers

221   **GHQ** General Head Quarters

221   **divagation** deviation or digression. McEwan's novel *Black Dogs* is claimed by its narrator to be a divagation

221   **Lord Gort** commander of the British Expeditionary Force

222   **strafing** shooting with machine guns from the air

223   **RAMC** Royal Army Medical Corps

225   **Messerschmitt** German fighter plane referred to on p. 223 as the ME 109

CONTEXT

To be disobedient or rude to an officer could result in a charge of insubordination and severe disciplining. This is why Robbie is surprised by Nettle and Mace's behaviour towards the major (p. 221).

PAGES 226–34

- Robbie keeps marching, passing more devastation.
- He reflects on why Briony might have said he raped Lola. He recalls an incident when, at ten years old, she made him save her from drowning, then declared her love for him.

As Robbie marches on, he revisits the sensual memories that have sustained him and thinks again of Cecilia's last letter with the promise it holds that Briony may retract her statement and enable him to clear his name. He falls to thinking of why she maintained so fervently that it was he who assaulted Lola, and reveals that he, too, is mistaken in his interpretation of events. He is convinced that Briony pursued the case with malice, having taken against him for some perceived slight. The only reason he can think of is that when she was ten she had played a dangerous trick, making him save her from drowning after a swimming lesson, in order to see a demonstration of how much he cared for her. She then told him she loved him, and he wonders if his rejection of her childish affections led her to harbour a grudge and plan a revenge against him. Briony later recalls this episode too (p. 342), and reveals that she had immediately forgotten about it after it happened.

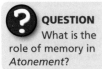

QUESTION
What is the role of memory in *Atonement*?

COMMENTARY

As Robbie recreates a summer day in England in his memory, it is a welcome relief from the marching and despair of the present, for us as well as for him. The idyllic picture of the pool in the woodland in summer, though rendered realistic by its dangerous currents and Briony's foolish act, is worlds away from the harsh realities of war-torn Normandy. There is a strange connection between the two, though, in the danger of death – then by drowning, now from war, and a few pages earlier from a swarm of bees – that is ever-present. The fragility of human existence is always close to the surface in this novel.

It is a sad **irony** that just as Briony misinterpreted Robbie's letter and embrace with Cecilia and found malice in them, so Robbie in his turn misinterprets Briony's testifying against him as malicious and vengeful. As he believes she deliberately lied in order to spite him, it is hardly surprising that he finds it impossible to forgive her. It is yet another facet of the novel's continuing exploration of how little a person can know of another's mind, how difficult it is to untangle actions and understand the motivation behind them or the connections between them.

Robbie considers, and we must agree, that the real, irreversible harm that has come to him as a result of the false conviction is that he cannot forgive and has passionately hated Briony, even fantasising about killing her with his bayonet. This hatred is born of his wrong belief that she deliberately lied. He recognises that it is an ugly change in his **character** and, like the lost years, cannot be undone.

GLOSSARY

234 **Wandsworth** Wandsworth prison, in south London, is one of the largest in Western Europe

---

PAGES 234–46

- The march continues.
- In another air attack, Robbie tries to protect a woman and her son, but finally has to abandon them. They are killed, but Robbie escapes to take cover in a wood.
- The three men carry on. They finally cross the bridge over the Bergues-Furnes canal but still have seven miles to go.

A column of French soldiers passes against the flow of the retreating British. Immediately after, another air attack starts. Robbie sees a woman with her six-year-old son and tries to help her. At first, she follows his lead but eventually will only sit on the ground and hug her child. Robbie has to abandon her and run, but is thrown off his feet by the blast. Parched and half-suffocated by the mud in his mouth, he makes his way into a wood. He sits there in a daze until Mace appears, bringing him water. Passing back through the field, Robbie sees a hole where the woman and child had been sitting and realises they have been completely vaporised by the blast.

The soldiers continue to trudge onwards, through banks of injured men, learning like everyone else to pay no heed to the cries for help. When they reach the bridge over the Bergues-Furnes canal they find that a sergeant is plucking soldiers from the rabble to work on

CONTEXT

Andre Maginot (1877–1932) was the French Minister for War from 1928–31. He gave his name to a defensive line of concrete bunkers built along France's border with Germany in the wake of the First World War. The German invasion of 1940 attacked France by bypassing the Maginot Line (mentioned on p. 234). By early June, Germany had cut off the Line, though it was still intact and some French commanders were keen to carry on defending it, even as France prepared to surrender.

CONTEXT

The incident on p. 240 of the two men operating the Norton motorcycle, one working the pedals and the other steering, is drawn from McEwan's father's experiences during the Second World War – injured in the legs, he shared a Harley-Davidson with a comrade whose arms were injured.

CHECK THE BOOK

W. H. Auden's poem 'Musée des Beaux Arts' comments on details of everyday life continuing through and around the horror of war, and includes the examples of a farmer ploughing his fields and a ship sailing on. Robbie has a copy of W. H. Auden's poems.

holding the perimeter against the advancing German army. Robbie limps, supported on either side by Mace and Nettle, to avoid being picked out by the sergeant. They can see planes attacking the troops waiting on the beaches for evacuation, and the number of wounded and dead by the roadside increases. Nettle throws away his boots, but Robbie persuades him to take them back and carry them. He has already prevented the two corporals throwing away their greatcoats – he knows they will be needed.

COMMENTARY

As the relentless marching and stream of horrors continues, Robbie, like everyone else, walks on past the injured. He asks 'What were they expected to do? Carry a dozen men on their backs when they could barely walk themselves?' (p. 245). It is true that he can do nothing to help, and there is so much suffering that any possible gesture would be lost in the enormity of the disaster. His own fatigue and his injury now make that gesture impossible. It is clear from his question that he feels guilty that he cannot help – he is defensive in proclaiming his impotence in the face of it all, and later he reflects on the extent of his own guilt (pp. 262–3).

The terrible scenes witnessed are thrown into relief and rendered yet more horrific by the fragments of everyday life glimpsed amongst them – the man ploughing and sheltering from the gunfire beneath a tree as though sheltering from rain (p. 235), the man and boys on the barge (p. 244) and, earlier, the woman and girl buying shoes (p. 216). Robbie is right that one day normal life will resume, that not everyone will be dead, but it is hard to believe in the midst of the chaos.

The true horror, too is revealed in the details. Like the severed leg in the tree, the fly-blown corpse is a focus of horror. Yet Robbie has become more resilient. He is still affected, but holds his breath as he goes past the corpse to retrieve Nettle's boot. For Nettle, he can still do something; but to feel for the corpse would be useless and would be to squander the dwindling resources of his remaining strength.

GLOSSARY

234	**detachment** a small unit detached from the main regiment
234	**tommies** English soldiers
234	*poilus* French soldiers (First World War term)
235	**Frogs** slang term for French people
236	**banshee** female spirit in Gaelic folklore known for horrendous wailing that presaged death
239	**Green Howards** Alexandra, Princess of Wales' Regiment; a Yorkshire rifle regiment in the British army
239	**Belgians have collapsed** after the defeat of their army the Belgians surrendered on 27 May 1940
239	**cordite** explosive containing cellulose nitrate
240	**Bray Dunes** seaside town with sand dunes near Dunkirk
240	**Norton** make of British-built motorbike
242	**Salvation Army** evangelical Christian movement organised along military lines; its social work includes tracing lost persons
242	**miasma** poisonous or unpleasant vapours
243	**howitzer** short-barrelled cannon with a steep angle of fire
243	**NAAFI** Navy, Army and Air Force Institutes; organisation providing food for British forces
243	**Coldstream Guards** Scottish infantry regiment in the British army
244	**BEF** British Expeditionary Force
244	**seed drill** device for planting seeds at well-spaced intervals

PAGES 246–65

- Robbie's mind is wandering as they finally make it into Dunkirk.
- Seeing the huge, disorganised mass of soldiers on the beach, Robbie, Mace and Nettle head for a bar. They rescue an RAF man who is about to be beaten up.

CONTEXT

'Each individual death is an explosion in itself, wrecking the lives of those nearest.' McEwan wrote these words of the 9/11 terrorist attacks, but he demonstrates the same idea in *Atonement*. He studied images from the conflict in Bosnia (1992–5) and drew on them in writing of the devastation in northern France.

- An old woman gives them food and drink in exchange for catching her escaped pig.
- Robbie and Nettle find a crowded cellar where they bed down and enjoy their meal in secret.
- Robbie's health worsens. Nettle wakes him as he is shouting in his sleep and annoying the other men. They are to rise at 7am for the evacuation.

Robbie drifts in and out of lucidity as exhaustion and the fever induced by his infected wound take their toll. When a neat-looking corporal forces Nettle to tie his boots and calls him a disgrace, Robbie reaches for his gun to shoot him, but luckily he has thrown it away (p. 239).

On the beach they find a disorganised rabble of thousands, lolling about and standing in the sea waiting; there are no boats. Robbie and his two companions head for a bar, but there is nothing to drink. A group of soldiers begins intimidating a lone RAF man, blaming him for the failure of the RAF to support the army. Violence erupts, and Robbie realises there is little time before the assault on the man becomes unstoppable. As he weighs up the possibilities, Mace rushes forwards and grabs the man. As Nettle and Robbie clear a path to the door, he carries the man out, saying he will drown him in the sea but intending to release him. The mob follows, but too late to find its rescued prey.

In a backstreet Robbie and Nettle ask an old woman for water. She demands that they first catch her pig and, though Nettle is reluctant, Robbie, in his delirium, is afraid she has power over his fate and agrees. In exchange she gives them good food and drink.

The soldiers look for somewhere to eat and sleep. In a bombed hotel, men are dragging out mattresses, but a squabble starts and several fall downstairs. One man is left screaming with a broken back, while others step over him. Robbie and Nettle find a place in a crowded cellar and enjoy their meal in secret.

CONTEXT

Many soldiers in the British army held the RAF responsible for heavy losses to German air raids. The Luftwaffe was better equipped than the RAF and supported the German ground troops efficiently, wiping out groups cut off by infantry and heavy artillery. The RAF did not present an organised response and, in 1940, had largely outmoded planes.

As Robbie's fever worsens, his mind drifts between past and present. He wonders about the guilt and innocence of everyone involved in the war, and he plans to go back to the cottage where he saw the leg and bury the boy. His mind is confused and rambling. Nettle wakes him because he is shouting, and tells him that the evacuation is in preparation. Robbie goes back to sleep.

COMMENTARY

The assault on the RAF man is horrific in its casual violence, its inevitability and its orchestration. The soldiers want to impress each other, to be applauded for their creativity in what they can think of doing to him. The man's helplessness goads them on and the attack develops a deadly momentum. Robbie is aware of the pattern it will take, having seen similar events in prison. He knows that he cannot simply step forward to speak out for the man as he will himself fall victim to the mob. He is too confused to formulate a plan, and even he is caught by the thrill of the moment, feeling 'unpleasantly excited' (p. 251). The episode is the more horrific and menacing because of the element of fun that is introduced into the account – the parallel with men enjoying a game of village cricket, the desire to maintain an elegant choreography with no discordant note. The heartlessness of the soldiers is repellent, but the RAF man does not defend himself by denying responsibility. Robbie suspects that if he spoke up the soldiers might be reminded of his humanity and brought to their senses. This seems a vain hope – the attack has its own dynamic and the people involved feel absolved of any individual responsibility.

Because Robbie's delirium is presented from his own point of view, the rationality of his actions and beliefs goes unquestioned. Only their strangeness, and Nettle's distrust of them, tell us that he is fevered. At the very end of the book, when the older Briony says that (perhaps) he died in Dunkirk of blood poisoning, we can look back to this delirium as a sure symptom of the coming end. Even so, his apparently mad decision to look for and trap the pig ends well, and Nettle's faith is restored.

The episode in the hotel is shocking. All the men have become so used to violence and death that the man with the broken back is

CHECK THE FILM

The opening scene of the film *A Clockwork Orange* (1971) uses a similar combination of terrible brutality, choreographed like art and presented to music by Beethoven. *A Clockwork Orange* was first released in the UK in 1972, but withdrawn in 1973. It was re-released with much publicity in 2000, when McEwan was writing *Atonement*. The central character is a fifteen-year-old boy who is drawn to violence to relieve the boredom of his life.

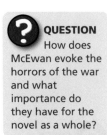

QUESTION
How does McEwan evoke the horrors of the war and what importance do they have for the novel as a whole?

CONTEXT
There is a long tradition of 'wise fools' in literature (both *King Lear* and *Twelfth Night* have one), and a popular tradition that mad people are blessed and sometimes mysteriously lucid or wise.

CHECK THE BOOK
The lines, *'Oh, when I was in love with you, Then I was clean and brave'*, quoted on p. 262, are from poem XVIII in A. E. Housman's *A Shropshire Lad* (1896).

ignored. As soon as it is established that he can't be helped, everyone simply steps over him and continues as before. Even Nettle and Robbie, who still have some compassion left, don't give him a second thought. Only we, as readers, will ever think of him again. How long will he lie there? Will anyone eventually move or kill him, or will he last for days, unhelped? He is a haunting reminder of the many senseless deaths of war, and a foretaste of the plight of the wounded that will be mercilessly scrutinised in Part Three.

Robbie's delirious ramblings about guilt and innocence, and his confusion of past events are not without their own wisdom and contain important reflections on the theme of guilt. His sad questioning of whether anyone is guiltless any more culminates in his aligning himself with Briony, whom he considers most guilty in his own life. 'We'll sleep it off, Briony' (p. 262), he says, indicating that he holds himself as guilty he believes her to be. Robbie has demonstrated considerable heroism and compassion in the course of Part Two, yet as he sinks further into illness and confusion he blames himself even for the death of the Flemish woman and her son who would not run from the air attack. It is a realistic evocation of how people in traumatic situations often feel responsible for things beyond their control, and contrasts with Briony's refusal of responsibility for her actions in Part One.

GLOSSARY

247	whaler small boat generally used in fairly shallow water
248	foxholes small pits dug for shelter from enemy fire
248	hour of the *passeggio* the practice of walking the streets (promenading) in the early evening
248	insouciant carefree
249	circles of suffering this refers to the circles of Hell in *The Divine Comedy*, written by Dante Alighieri (1265–1321). Sinners are allocated to a circle according to their sins, with different punishments in each
249	pissoir urinal

GLOSSARY CONTINUED

250   **Mile End Road**   main street in the East End of London

250   **Sauchiehall Street**   main street in Glasgow, Scotland's second city

251   **Spitfires and Hurricanes**   planes used by the RAF in the Second World War

253   **Johnny Weissmuller's Tarzan**   Johnny Weissmuller was the star of a string of Tarzan movies, beginning with *Tarzan the Ape Man* in 1932

254   **where the night was rising**   as the sun sets in the west, the sky in the east becomes dark first

259   **chenille**   thick, soft, tufted fabric

259   **chaise longue**   a narrow couch with an arm at one end and a back extending only part way along, for a single person to recline on

264   **gunwale**   (pronounced 'gunnel') the top of the side of a boat

---

PART THREE

PAGES 269–77

- Briony is a nurse probationer.
- She observes changes at the hospital but does not know that they are preparations for war.

For this part of the novel, the narrative remains located in 1940 but has moved from France back to England where Briony is a trainee nurse in a London hospital.

Briony's life is a round of menial tasks that she has to learn and repeat endlessly. She suffers under the stern authority of Sister Drummond and the strict regime of hard, physical work. Most of her time is spent cleaning. Briony's life is beset with apparently petty rules and regulations that, like army training, are designed to instil absolute, unquestioning obedience.

 CHECK THE NET

For a firsthand account of London during the Second World War, go to **www. eyewitnesstohistory. com** and type 'London 1939' into the search engine.

She has noticed that the wards are emptying and new supplies are turning up, including extra beds which have to be thoroughly cleaned.

COMMENTARY

The regulations that seem petty to Briony recall some of the army activity we have glimpsed in Part Two. The stones painted white outside the hut on the perimeter of Dunkirk are a sign of one of the pointless tasks that occupy the army in less desperate times. In nursing, lining up the patients' noses with the creases in their sheets is a manifestation of the same mentality. The ward discipline, like the stone-painting, will give way to some degree in the coming onslaught. But the benefit of the training in unquestioning obedience will become clear, too, as Briony comes to rely on routine to carry her through the emotional trauma of dealing with war casualties.

Briony is not sure what to expect, but from the opening of this part of the novel it is clear that something is imminent. The swollen, turbulent river is a symbol of the state of the hospital and the whole city: both rise in 'unease' (p. 269). Something is growing, and soon it will burst upon them. There is a clue in the extra beds, which spread 'like deaths in the night' (p. 270), and the ominously large supplies of morphine, a powerful painkiller.

Briony's writing style is more assured and her new maturity is clear in her voice, changed markedly since the first part of the novel. The self-consciously literary posturings of the very young writer have given way to poised and evocative prose, unhurried and confident. Long sentences that make use of the best – rather than superficially impressive – words make it a style that is easy to read and unobtrusive. We learn later (p. 277) that Briony writes an account of her days at the hospital in her notebooks, and presumably it is on these that the older Briony, as novelist, draws. The style captures the immediacy of the observed routine and experience with the eloquence of the older writer.

Again, Briony finds herself thrown together with a girl of her own age, not of her own choosing. Her new companion, Fiona (who sleeps in the next bed), resembles Lola in having ginger hair and freckles, but is otherwise very different from Lola. The detail of her

CONTEXT

The surname of one of Briony's fellow probationers, Susan Langland, is shared with medieval poet William Langland who spent much of his life reworking a single poem, *Piers Plowman*, which sought to show a way to salvation.

asking Briony to cut the fingernails on her right hand, a childish incompetence revealing her dependence on her mother, is in sharp contrast with Lola's attempts to be worldly and grown up. Fiona is completely without guile, makes no attempt to pretend to be anything she is not and does not intimidate Briony in the least. 'Loud and jolly' (p. 273), Fiona is from Chelsea and her father is apparently a politician, so she has similar social standing to Briony. Briony finds in her a cheerful and unchallenging ally and she becomes her friend by default (p. 274).

Briony's new life is very different from the leisured privilege of her childhood, and the continuation of it that she had expected at Girton, following in Cecilia's footsteps. She expresses no resentment at the rigours of nursing, nor does she glorify the hardships to elevate her status as a martyr and penitent. In the first hint that she is paying the price for actions in the first part of the novel, she reveals only that she 'was delivered from introspection' (p. 276), the hard work and lack of time saving her from thinking about what she has done. The only clue that Briony may be disappointed with the exchange – studying at Cambridge for working in the hospital – is in her reflection that 'she thought she was joining the war effort' (p. 275) but has ended up a skivvy commanded by Sister Drummond. This, though, is soon to change as her contribution to the war becomes very real.

GLOSSARY	
270	**La Coupole** dance club and bar in Boulevard Montparnasse, Paris
272	**carbolised** cleaned with carbolic acid (phenol)
272	**autoclaves** ovens for sterilising equipment
272	**Bunyan Bags** bags used to encase burned limbs, which are kept floating in saline (salt solution)
274	**Chelsea** area of south-west London
274	**Churchill** British political leader during most of the Second World War, from 1940
274	**VADs** members of the Voluntary Aid Detachment which provided medical care during the First and Second World Wars
276	**Bovril** hot drink made with beef extract

CHECK THE BOOK

For an entertaining and informative history of women and war look at Kate Adie's book, *Corsets to Camouflage* (Hodder and Stoughton, 2004).

> **GLOSSARY CONTINUED**
>
> 277 **gentian violet** violet solution used as an antiseptic and in the treatment of burns
>
> 277 **ringworm** fungal infection of the skin
>
> 277 **aquaflavine emulsion** yellow liquid used to prevent bacterial infection of wounds
>
> 277 **lead lotion** astringent which shrinks blood vessels, reducing the subcutaneous bleeding that produces bruises

PAGES 277–86

- In bed, Briony writes her journal, making up or embellishing some of the details. She reflects on letters from home and the news they bring.
- From a newspaper report, Briony realises that the hospital is preparing for the wounded from Dunkirk.
- She receives a letter from her father telling her that Lola and Paul Marshall are to marry.

CONTEXT

Many types of food and some other goods were rationed during the Second World War. Each person was issued with a book of vouchers and had to hand over a voucher when buying restricted goods. It was not possible to buy more than the allowed ration in a week.

Briony's letters home are perfunctory and share none of her daily life. This she records in her journal. From her parents she hears that three families of evacuees have been sent to the house, and one of the evacuee children has broken the statue in the fountain. Local railings have been torn up to be melted down to make more planes for the war effort. Danny Hardman has joined the navy.

Before starting her training, Briony spent time living with an aunt and uncle in London and typed her first attempt at a story based around the events described in Part One of *Atonement*. She sent her story to a literary journal, *Horizon*, but has had no reply. She has also written to Cecilia – this is the letter we have already heard about in Cecilia's letter to Robbie (pp. 211–13) – but as yet has had no reply from her sister either.

Clearing up newspapers, Briony discovers that the British army is retreating to Dunkirk and realises that the preparations at the hospital are for the casualties from the defeat in France, and perhaps even from an imminent invasion of Britain. She tries to phone her father at his ministry, but is unable to get through to him.

COMMENTARY

It is ironic that Briony finds the other girls theatrical in their homesickness, as over-dramatising has been a feature of Briony's own character in the early part of *Atonement*. It highlights the changes in Briony herself. Another change is that she has gone from craving her mother's attention to withholding details of her new life from her parents. The letters from home make her feel nostalgic, but for us the concerns of her family look petty in contrast with the terrible events that Robbie has experienced and witnessed, and the horrific injuries that Briony will soon see. The literal destruction of parts of the family's country estate echoes the destruction of an era in English social history that the estate represents.

In Briony's account of her journal we glimpse the old Briony, still thinking she will become a great writer. She considers that 'she was really an important writer in disguise' (p. 280) – a childish turn of phrase that reminds us that she is still only eighteen in this section. Her thoughts about literature have changed, though. Now she hopes to be part of a new direction in English writing, one in which plot and **character** have given way to something else. The **modernist** writing of the early decades of the twentieth century has impressed Briony and she sees this as the way forward. But she has gone overboard in her enthusiasm for impressionistic writing. (There is more about this in the section **Themes: Writing and imagination**.) Another reminder that Briony is still very young comes with her surprise at realising the retreat to Dunkirk lies behind the preparations at the hospital, and her sudden desire to speak to her father.

CONTEXT

The Nightingale School for Nurses in London was founded in 1860 by Florence Nightingale (1820–1910). It was the first nursing college in the world and marked the start of nursing as a trained profession. It was run on strict lines adapted from military discipline, as Florence Nightingale had developed her practices at Scutari during the Crimean War (1854–6).

GLOSSARY

278	**evacuees** young children who had been evacuated from the cities – sent to live in the countryside in order to avoid injury from German bombing raids
278	**billeted** sent to live with
278	**requisitioned** commandeered by the military

GLOSSARY CONTINUED

278   **Nice** city in the south of France, on the French Riviera

279   **pillbox** small, cylindrical fortification

279   **teal** small duck

279   **grey wagtails** small birds with a grey back and yellow under-tail; they wag their tails up and down

279   **gas mask** protective mask to be used in the event of a poisonous gas attack

279   **ARP warden** Air Raid Precaution warden; civilians trained to help people during air raids (aerial bomb attacks). They were also responsible for checking that people did not show a light after dark and carried their gas mask

279   **Primrose Hill** district of London near Regent's Park

280   **manifestos** documents declaring intentions, aims and policy

280   **Chaucer** the poet Geoffrey Chaucer (c. 1342–1400); author of *The Canterbury Tales*, a collection of stories in verse told by pilgrims walking to Canterbury. The pilgrims are vividly drawn portraits of people from all walks of life

280   **coves, topers, old hats** slang terms for good fellows (coves), people who drink too much (topers) and people with a lot of experience (old hats)

281   **dispensary** place where medicine is handed out

281   **ampersands** the character '&', meaning 'and'

281   *Horizon* literary journal founded by Cyril Connolly and the poet Stephen Spender, published c. 1939–c. 50

282   **jaundice** disease characterised by yellow skin, resulting from bile pigments in the blood

283   **Big Ben** bell of the clock in St Stephen's Tower at the northern end of the Houses of Parliament, Westminster

283   **sputum mugs** mugs to spit into

283   **haemorrhages** episodes of internal bleeding

284   *Sunday Graphic* tabloid Sunday newspaper

284   **surrender of the Dutch army** the Netherlands surrendered on 15 May 1940, the day after the carpet-bombing of Rotterdam

284   **euphemism** inoffensive word or phrase used instead of a more controversial term

285   **almoner** hospital social worker

286   **Westminster Bridge** bridge over the River Thames in Westminster, London. It goes between the Houses of Parliament and the South Bank

CONTEXT

The Dutch city of Rotterdam was bombed on 14 May 1940 after a breakdown in communications in German army command. The assault, planned for 13:20, had been delayed until 16:20 to allow for negotiations, but the attack fleet set off at the original time and bombed the city, killing 800–900 people.

PAGES 287–315

- The nurses are given a half day off and Briony goes with Fiona to the park. On their return, they find the front of the hospital crowded with army vehicles and injured soldiers.

- Briony feels inadequate as she struggles with the first tasks she is given, only partially succeeding at them.

- Her confidence increases as she deals successfully with several disturbing injuries.

- Arriving at her room in the early hours of the morning, Briony finds a letter from the editor of *Horizon* refusing her story but with an encouraging commentary.

The nurses do not know why they have been given half the day off, but Briony and Fiona go to St James's Park to enjoy it. When they return to the hospital, the forecourt is crowded with injured soldiers, with more being unloaded from army vehicles. Briony and Fiona run across, just as staff come out from the hospital, and are drawn into work immediately.

Briony takes one end of a stretcher, but can only just carry it to the ward and finally lets it slip. The jolt is painful for the wounded soldier and Briony feels she has failed. Her feelings of inadequacy mount as she makes minor mistakes in other tasks. She finally feels better about herself when Sister Drummond compliments her on how well she has cleaned a soldier's wounded leg.

Her next task is to removal shrapnel from a man's leg. When he yells an expletive, Sister Drummond tells him off. Briony continues, ending with a piece of shrapnel four inches long that takes three attempts to pull free. Briony goes away to get him some brandy and is sick.

Briony is asked to dress a soldier who has lost half his face. It is a task she has dreaded, though now she is more afraid of the reproach she sees in his eyes than of the sight of the wounds. Her next task is aborted, as the burnt soldier is too badly injured for her to do anything for him and he soon dies. Later she is sent to talk to a

---

CONTEXT

It was illegal to show any light from windows after dark during the war. By cutting light from all buildings, the British government hoped to make it difficult for German bombers to spot and bomb cities at night time. Thick, black fabric was used to cover windows to avoid any light escaping. The fabric and the action of hiding all light were both called 'black out'.

CONTEXT

Basil Liddell Hart (1895–1970) was a British military historian and strategist. He analysed the history of the First World War to discover why so many soldiers died and developed a strategy more likely to be successful in another was. The book by Liddell Hart mentioned on p. 288 is probably *The Defence of Britain*, published in 1939.

French boy who is dying of head injuries. At first she is offended, thinking she has been sent to chat to him because she is tired, yet it turns out to be the hardest task of all. The boy is confused, sometimes rambling incoherently and sometimes confusing Briony with a girl from his home village. Briony is initially confused herself, as he seems to know about her family. At first she tries to correct him, but once she discovers the extent of his injuries and sees that he cannot survive she pretends to be the girl he remembers.

Back in her room, Briony opens a letter from the editor of *Horizon*. The letter is a critique of Briony's story about the incident at the fountain between Robbie and Cecilia. Some of the earlier part of *Atonement* is recognisable from Connolly's comments. In the letter, the editor rejects the story for publication, but encourages Briony to send in more writing or visit the offices of *Horizon*.

COMMENTARY

This section is unrelenting in its horror. From the cheerful, sunny start, we and Briony are suddenly plunged into a hellish nightmare of terrible suffering and horrific injuries. The first incident, carrying the stretcher, is a shock to Briony. She is not physically strong enough to do it. Then she flounders, losing a troupe of men with crutches, and inappropriately tries to make soldiers get out of bed because she thinks she has to follow the right procedures. She is silently defensive when she realises the rules that have been drummed into her have been abandoned. But once she gets into her stride, she copes well. The voice of cheery authority comes easily, and she is able to press on with terrifying procedures despite trembling and feeling sick.

The style of the writing does nothing to diminish the horror. There are several images drawn from familiar, domestic settings – the blackened leg like an over-ripe banana, the removal of blood-caked gauze likened to whipping a tablecloth from beneath crockery. The **juxtaposition** of the homely, comforting images with the men's agony throws the latter into sharp relief, making it all the more awful. When Briony is sick in the sluice, it is mentioned as if in passing, with no emphasis and no hint of sympathy, making the point that this is nothing beside what the men on the ward must endure.

CONTEXT

The initials 'CC' that are used to sign Briony's letter presumably stand for Cyril Connolly (1903–74), an influential English critic and writer. He founded and edited the literary journal *Horizon*, which was published from c.1939 to c.1950.

Briony's last three patients have increasingly horrific injuries: each time we believe it cannot get any worse, and then find it does. The patients' reactions are as effective as the description of their injuries in conjuring up the terrible extent of what has happened to them. Each is realised as a person, from Private Latimer's disappointed sound which is such a massive understatement of his plight, to the wandering, confused French boy whose history is revealed in snatches. These are real, wrecked people, not statistics and not like the illustrations in the clinical books which have been Briony's only previous exposure to the details of anatomy.

Briony adapts quickly. After the death of the French boy, the most devastating scene in the novel, she washes, changes her clothes and returns to work on the wards – though nothing she does afterwards warrants description. Even the senior, experienced nurses are out of their depth with the war wounded. Empathy cuts through the formality and orderliness which is still maintained. The accounts of the injuries are so obscene, blatant and graphic that the text becomes emotionally devastating to read and we, as readers, are also exhausted by the experience. Briony 'learned a simple, obvious thing she had always known, and everyone knew' (p. 304) – in this one night she comes to understand the sheer fragility of the human body in a way she could not begin to apprehend before.

The letter from Cyril Connolly addresses very different concerns and returns us to the Briony of the first part of the novel, the would-be writer. It is a curious passage, a detailed critique of a piece of writing we do not see but which has formed the basis of the early part of *Atonement*. Some phrases are still in the final novel; some details are different and the whole section describing the events round the fountain has been recast, following Connolly's suggestion, as a specific interlude in a larger piece with more **narrative** development. There is a more detailed account of this passage in the **Extended commentaries** and, in the **Literary background** section, a discussion of *Atonement*'s relation to early twentieth-century literature.

CONTEXT

McEwan has spoken about his vivid depictions of violence and its consequences: '[In writing about violence] you've got to embrace it, you've got to make your reader … *see*. So, when people accuse me of being too graphic in my depictions of violence, my response is, "Well, either you *do* violence, or you sentimentalise it" ' (Interview with Jonathan Noakes; Margaret Reynolds and Jonathan Noakes, *Ian McEwan: The Child in Time, Enduring Love, Atonement* (Vintage, 2002), pp. 22–3).

 CHECK THE BOOK

Dusty Answer is a novel by Rosamund Lehmann (1901–90), published in 1927. *Atonement* has echoes of its concerns and writing style. Lehmann's work explores the female consciousness in the inter-war years.

PART THREE PAGES 287–315 continued

CONTEXT

The French philosopher Henri Bergson (1859–1941) distinguished two levels of consciousness, one reached by deep introspection which is the seat of creativity and freewill, the other an outward expression of this. He won the Nobel Prize for Literature in 1927.

CONTEXT

On p. 313, three different types of valuable porcelain are referred to. Ming is Chinese porcelain produced during the Ming dynasty (1368–1644). Sèvres was produced at the town of Sèvres near Versailles, France, from 1756, superseding Meissen as the most desirable in Europe. Nymphenburg is a German porcelain, produced near Munich from 1747 and copying the styles of Meissen.

GLOSSARY

287 **Elgar** Sir Edward Elgar (1857–1934), English composer who began a renaissance in English music. His music is bold and tuneful

287 **air-raid shelters** underground shelters in which people hid from aerial bombardments

287 **man in armband and cap** an ARP warden; in the first part of the war, ARP wardens and the police were charged with stopping people who did not appear to be carrying their gas masks

287 **soft-skulled babies** in very young babies, the bones of the skull are not fused, leaving two soft, unprotected spots between plates of the skull (fontanelles)

291 **casualty-receiving stations** injured men had wounds dressed near the battlefield and were then sent to a receiving station from which they were directed to proper hospital facilities according to their needs

291 **triage** initial assessment of medical conditions

295 **vacolitres** bags of fluid used with a drip or for blood transfusions

295 **plasma** yellowish fluid extracted from blood by removing the red and white blood cells

295 **gangrene** death and decay of body tissue as a result of injury or interrupted flow of blood

298 **forceps** surgical pincers, looking rather like scissors

302 **eusol** solution of chlorinated lime and boric acid used to remove dead and rotting tissue from wounds

302 **tannic acid** used in the treatment of burns until the mid 1940s; it reduces toxic products from burn injuries, reduces pain and helps to prevent infection

305 **'Te voilà enfin'** 'Here you are at last'

309 **Causse de Larzac** area of dramatic landscape in the Dordogne area of France

312 **Mrs Woolf** the novelist Virginia Woolf (1882–1941)

313 **thrown the baby … water** from the idiom to 'throw the baby out with the bathwater' (see **Extended commentaries**)

314 **Piazza Navona** square in Rome with a fountain by Bernini, the Fontana dei fiumi (fountain of the rivers)

314 **mulched** a mulch is a layer of partly composted vegetable matter spread on the soil to enrich it

PAGES 315–27

- After the initial chaos, the hospital routine slows down a little, and Briony works regular, thirteen-hour shifts. She becomes increasingly aware, however, of the expected, imminent invasion by the German army.
- Briony makes her way to the church where Paul and Lola are getting married and slips inside to watch.
- She considers objecting to their marriage, but does not do so. She now realises it was Paul who attacked Lola on the island.

Relieved by the return of some kind of normal routine in the hospital, Briony has time to anticipate the German invasion that everyone believes is about to happen. For her, everything she observes is brought sharply into focus as she imagines its imminent destruction by the invading forces. This lends urgency to her plan to visit her sister.

Briony feels vulnerable and clumsy as she makes her way across London with an ancient map. Despite her recent experiences, she is still immature in her relation to the world outside. Showing some of her characteristic theatricality, she fantasises that people may think her a spy.

There are few guests in the modest church – only the immediate families of Lola and Paul. Although she wants to stand up and say that she knows a reason they should not marry, she cannot find adequate words or reason. She reveals that she now knows that Paul assaulted Lola, and that in their marriage the secret of it is locked away forever. Lola seems to recognise her and frown, but of the other guests only the twins know who she is. She allows them all to leave before she goes outside herself.

COMMENTARY

Although Briony has been exposed to much in the hospital, outside she is anxious. The strict routine and rule of the hospital have robbed her of any confidence in acting for herself. The threat of an impending invasion, as well as the outlandish possibility that people

> **CONTEXT**
>
> On the orders of the government, street names and signs were painted over and maps were not available. The intention was to make it as difficult as possible for any invading troops to find their way around.

> **CONTEXT**
>
> Elizabeth Bowen (1899–1973) was an Anglo-Irish novelist and short story writer. Her style is finely wrought and her stories tell of difficult relationships amongst the English upper-middle classes – she could easily have been a model for Briony's writing.

will think her a spy, are fuel for her active imagination. It is in her imagination, too, that she stands up to proclaim an objection to the marriage. In fact, she cannot formulate a good reason – and the rape and subsequent wrongful conviction are not reasons against the marriage. The false account of her walking up the aisle to denounce the marriage is a foreshadowing of the later revelation that the end of Part Three is also untrue (p. 370).

This is the first time we learn that Briony has decided that Paul committed the assault. Until this point, we have probably believed that the scratches and bruises Lola revealed to Briony in her bedroom were inflicted by the twins, and the revelation that it was Paul Marshall is shocking. Also disturbing is the imagery Briony uses of the secret, walled-up alive in their marriage. It is an inauspicious start to married life but, as the final instalment of the novel reveals, the secret gives the Marshalls' relationship strength against the outside world. In fact, there are no positive depictions of marriage in the novel. Emily and Jack share a hollow partnership, he having a long-term affair and she denying knowledge of it. Emily's sister Hermione is in the process of divorcing her husband in Part One. This marriage between Paul and Lola, barely celebrated, hides a dark secret and binds them together as partners in crime. There is no suggestion that the only true lovers, Cecilia and Robbie, may marry.

CONTEXT

The Home Guard was a defence force drawn from male volunteers not drafted into the army. It was formed on 14 May 1940 and grew within days to number many thousands of men as there was great enthusiasm for it. It was sometimes criticised for being disorganised and amateurish, the men armed with whatever weapons fell to hand.

GLOSSARY

317	**blooded** initiated; the expression is from hunting, when young huntsmen were smeared with blood from the killed animal after attending their first successful hunt
318	**Lambeth Palace** official residence of the Archbishop of Canterbury, on the bank of the Thames in London
321	**tonsure** hairstyle worn by monks, where the crown of the head is shaved but hair grows in a ring around it
321	**draymen** men who drive a dray, a low horse-drawn cart for carrying heavy loads
322	**confluence** coming together
324	**tulle and organdie** tulle is a light-weight netting, often made of silk and used for bridal veils; organdie is a stiffened, transparent silk fabric

GLOSSARY CONTINUED

324	**morning suit** suit comprising a tail coat, trousers and a shirt with a wing collar worn for weddings and formal court occasions
325	**Assize Court** court convened periodically in various parts of England to hear cases of serious crime; abolished in England in 1971
325	**All Souls, Oxford** All Souls College at the University of Oxford

PAGES 328–49

- Briony goes to Cecilia's house in Balham. Cecilia is not pleased to see her. Robbie is also there and is extremely hostile.
- Briony tells them that the assault on Lola was committed by Paul Marshall, and that he and Lola have married.
- Briony agrees to make a new statement, write to Robbie explaining all that happened and visit her parents to explain to them.
- She ends determined to write a new draft of the whole story, to atone for what she has done.

Briony is on her way to see her sister, though we do not immediately know where she is heading. Reluctant to get there too quickly, she stops for breakfast in an unpleasant café. When she arrives, she encounters a hostile landlady, and a no less hostile Cecilia. Her sister has little interest in her news from home, except for the information that Betty has broken Uncle Clem's vase. It is clear that the rim Cecilia mended broke away while Betty was carrying it, and Betty was unjustly blamed for the accident which in fact resulted from Cecilia's actions – a tiny parallel to Briony's own guilt.

When Robbie discovers that Briony is there, he is furious and can barely contain himself. Briony sees Cecilia calm him in the same way that she used to calm Briony as a child. There is still misunderstanding, as Briony does not know that Cecilia and Robbie, in their own misinterpretation of events, have blamed Danny Hardman for the assault and built up an unfounded hatred towards him. They are shocked to learn that Paul was the rapist, and

CONTEXT

The phrase, 'Lady Muck' (p. 334), means a woman with social pretensions. McEwan, in his essay, 'Mother tongue' (*Guardian*, 13 October 2001), recalls how his mother jokingly referred to herself as Lady Muck once. It is possible that it is included as a tribute to her.

CONTEXT

The wallpaper, striped 'like a boy's pyjamas' (p. 335), recalls the leg and scraps of pyjama fabric at the start of Part Two and, their bar-like pattern which 'heightened the sense of confinement', recalls Robbie's time in prison. Both are shadowy reminders of Robbie before he comes into the room.

just as shocked and angry to find that Paul and Lola have married. Robbie instructs Briony to swear an oath, write him an explanation and tell her parents the true version of events. He and Cecilia then escort Briony to the underground station so that they can spend their last hour together before Robbie rejoins his regiment. Briony anticipates writing her new account which will be her atonement for her error.

COMMENTARY

This is both the end of the main part of the novel and its beginning, as Briony determines to write a new version of the story, 'an atonement' (p. 349), which will eventually become the novel we have just read. The signature, 'BT / London 1999' (p. 349), is the first indication that the whole book has been written by Briony in old age. This realisation inevitably colours our appreciation of all that has gone before, demanding that we re-evaluate our reading of the novel immediately.

Cecilia and Robbie have both changed. Made sterner by passing time and their terrible experiences, they have lost the excitement and optimism of early adulthood. They are no longer embarking on an exciting journey, but surviving a gruelling life. The hazy, languid days of Part One are a long way off – there is a sense that the early part of the novel was unreal but that now everyone, including Briony, has grown up and this is what existence really is. The love between Robbie and Cecilia is an adult, sustaining love. The fierce urgency of passion they displayed in the library is recalled in the harsh physicality with which Cecilia draws Robbie back from the brink of violence against Briony.

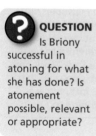

QUESTION

Is Briony successful in atoning for what she has done? Is atonement possible, relevant or appropriate?

By contrast, there is still something of the naïve child in Briony. She keeps hoping for some reconciliation, forgiveness or even a sign that this will be possible in the future. She imagines she could regain her 'post of beloved younger sister' (p. 329).

Briony's experiences as a nurse have given her enough insight to see that she will never be able to see what Robbie has seen, feel as he feels – and yet in writing her story, she has shown us his experiences and feelings. This is a comment on the right and obligation of the novelist to delve into the psyche of **characters** they have created but at the same time recognises that ultimately each person is knowable only to him or herself. Fiction requires that the writer is able to imagine as fully as possible what it is like to be someone else, and helps the reader to do the same. Empathising with others is the key to understanding and enjoying literature.

That Robbie and Cecilia have also clung to an inaccurate version of the events in 1935 is not only **ironic**, but contributes to the continuing theme of truth and memory. Their certainty that Danny Hardman was guilty, with no more evidence than Briony had for believing Robbie to be guilty, lessens her guilt by removing its uniqueness. It is only a combination of circumstances that has turned Briony's mistaken belief into a catastrophe, while Robbie and Cecilia's mistaken belief has no significant consequences at all.

The ending is hopeful. Briony is still holding on to her naïve belief that she can make things better in some way, and Cecilia and Robbie are happy together. This is all to be undermined in the epilogue – the illusion of balance and resolution will be torn away and we will have to make our own decisions about what to believe.

> **CONTEXT**
>
> McEwan has said that the ability to imagine what it is like to be someone else is the root of compassion and morality: 'It is hard to be cruel once you permit yourself to enter the mind of your victim. Imagining what it is like to be someone other than yourself is at the core of our humanity ...' ('Only love and then oblivion ...', *Guardian*, 15 September 2001).

GLOSSARY

328	**asphalt**	black road surface made from a sticky, bitumen-based substance mixed with gravel
329	**stone drinking trough**	in streets, these were for horses to drink at
329	**hypoglycaemia**	low blood sugar level causing symptoms such as light-headedness, trembling and perspiration
330	**Ford 8**	popular two-door saloon car of the 1930s
331	**inauspicious**	presaging bad luck
331	**valves**	before the invention of transistors, radios were powered by glass valves which took some time to warm up
333	**sardonic**	mocking or sarcastic
339	**egg powder**	during the war, fresh eggs were not widely available; a powder made from dried eggs was used instead

LONDON, 1999

PAGES 353–71

- In old age, Briony faces the prospect of losing her mind to dementia.
- Visiting the Imperial War Museum Library, she sees Paul and Lola from a distance.
- She goes to the old Tallis house for her seventy-seventh birthday celebration and watches a performance of *The Trials of Arabella*.
- Briony has rewritten her story many times. This version is the first in which Cecilia and Robbie live to be reunited.

CONTEXT

The account McEwan gives on pp. 354–5 is not particularly characteristic of either vascular dementia or Alzheimer's Disease. Diagnosing vascular dementia only by a brain scan is unreliable as irregularities are common in people of this age and do not necessarily indicate stroke damage. A better distinction is between the steady decline of Alzheimer's and the alternating periods of lucidity and rapid deterioration in vascular dementia. The description Briony gives of the expected pattern of decline does not suit either vascular dementia or Alzheimer's, particularly the involvement of the autonomous nervous system.

The elderly Briony is tidying her papers at the end of her last retelling of her tale, which has become *Atonement*. She has vascular dementia, a degenerative brain condition that will lead to the loss of memory and then all other faculties and functions until she dies in a few years' time.

On the morning of her seventy-seventh birthday, Briony goes to the Imperial War Museum Library to deposit some letters from Nettle. As she arrives, she sees Paul and Lola leaving, but avoids meeting them. Though Paul is old and frail, Lola is sprightly. Briony reflects on their charity over the years, wondering whether they have been trying to atone for their own crime. They also have a reputation for being litigious, and Briony realises that as Lola will outlive her, it will be impossible for her to publish her novel in her own lifetime.

A minicab collects Briony to take her to her childhood home, now converted to a hotel. We learn a few details about the later lives of some of the **characters** from Part One of the novel. Pierrot has organised a performance by the assembled children of Briony's **melodrama**, *The Trials of Arabella*, which they watch in the library. Alone in her room, Briony reflects on how she has represented history, and makes the stunning revelation that this is the first time she has allowed the lovers to survive until the end of the book. She suggests that, in fact, Robbie died in France and Cecilia in the Blitz.

COMMENTARY

The epilogue is remarkable in unpicking all that has gone before. The contract that we have entered into with the novelist, to believe in the events narrated, is now void. The story is at an end, and Briony steps back to tell us how much was true, and to stun us with her rewriting of the ending. In saying that she can see no virtue in presenting the bleak 'true' end of Robbie and Cecilia's history she is returning to her earlier position of wanting a balanced and satisfying story, one 'sealed off at both ends so it resembled … every other story in the world' (p. 6). Briony, of course, has not now done this as the epilogue undermines her construct.

The reversal raises the questions of what a reader wants and expects from a novel, what the novelist is under an obligation to deliver and whether the **narrator** has any duty to truth. The complex issues of memory and truth, woven throughout the novel, are given another unexpected twist by the news that Briony is losing her mind and that soon all will be lost beyond recall. (There is more about this in **Themes: Memory and truth** and **Writing and imagination**.)

We see many of the characters from the first part of the novel, ravaged by age. It is an unpleasant shock to see Leon in his wheelchair, paralysed by a stroke, Paul Marshall frail and Briony on the brink of degeneration. Lola is fiercely defiant of old age, with a slightly frightening energy that is perhaps born of decades of protecting and denying the secret at the heart of her marriage.

The Tallis house is changed, but Briony is barely nostalgic for it, having already renounced it as her home long ago. Its new name, Tilney's, takes us back to the quotation from *Northanger Abbey* before the beginning of the novel. The glimpses of other characters' histories – Leon's marriages and the early death of his first wife, the deaths of Jackson and Emily, Briony's own marriage to a Frenchman, her father's second marriage – all hint at other stories that could have been told. But just as we might be believing in this final, outer, fiction, Briony/McEwan undermines it again with the suggestion that she could rewrite even the epilogue and put Robbie and Cecilia in the library watching the play. We end with the sense that we do not know what is real; we can never know 'what *really*

> **CONTEXT**
>
> McEwan has referred to Leo Tolstoy's (1828–1910) 'crucial question', as being relevant to Briony's concern that all is lost in death: 'My question – that which at the age of fifty brought me to the verge of suicide – was the simplest of questions, lying in the soul of every man … Is there any meaning in my life that the inevitable death awaiting me does not destroy' (*A Confession*, Part V).

CONTEXT

Shakespeare sometimes allows an authority figure to step out of the fiction at the end of a play and draw attention to the fact that it was all play-acting, all made up. This happens in *The Tempest*, *A Midsummer Night's Dream* and *Twelfth Night*, for example.

happened' (p. 371). In stepping back, Briony prompts us to reflect that perhaps the whole story was all made up after all.

GLOSSARY

353 **Bedlam** a hospital for the mentally ill, dating back to 1247. In the eighteenth century patients were exhibited to paying visitors

354 **vascular dementia** the second most common form of dementia, after Alzheimer's Disease

354 **Alzheimer's** Alzheimer's Disease, the principal cause of dementia. Mental faculties diminish steadily over time, beginning with memory lapses

355 **autonomous nervous system** part of the nervous system that controls essential body functions such as heartbeat, breathing, digestion and temperature

355 **Morgon** red wine from the Beaujolais region of France

355 **Let me not be mad** quotation from Shakespeare's *King Lear*: 'O! Let me not be mad, not mad, sweet heaven; keep me in temper; I would not be mad!' (I.5.46–7)

356 **panoply** magnificent array

357 **plutocrat** ruler who has power by dint of being wealthy

358 **the side … buttered** the most advantageous position or choice

358 **Cruella de Vil** female villain in the novel *101 Dalmatians* by Dodie Smith. In the 1996 Disney film, Cruella de Vil is the owner of a fashion design house and dresses in very stylish, if eccentric, clothes

359 **irascible** easily angered; irritable

361 **dévoré** velvet fabric on which a raised pattern is produced by dissolving some of the pile

363 **giant elms lost to disease** Dutch Elm Disease killed most of the elm trees in the UK during the 1960s

367 **glottal 't'** a 't' which is not pronounced, leaving a hiatus in a word

370 **unhappy inversion** Briony means that the reversal of 'we sail into the sunset' is not pleasing

371 **atheists** people who reject belief in God

EXTENDED COMMENTARIES

TEXT 1 – PART ONE, CHAPTER 1 (PP. 5–6)

From 'But hidden drawers ...' to '... when he was at home.'

The first chapter of the novel introduces Briony's **character** at thirteen years of age. The way that Briony is presented here will affect how we see her and judge her actions. Even though there will be a chance to reappraise this picture in the light of coming events, the first introduction to a character makes a lasting impression. What is revealed about Briony in these pages, therefore, carries a lot of weight.

The voice describing Briony appears to be that of an **omniscient narrator** who has privileged insights into her mental state. A sense of Briony's own dissatisfaction with her unexciting life comes through, though. That no one wanted to know about the squirrel's skull sounds like the sulky complaint of a petulant child. This method of presenting a character's own views or realm of consciousness by giving the narrator words or turns of phrase that could be the character's own is used throughout *Atonement*. The language holds a lot of pent-up energy and potential for disaster. Even though the text is saying that these things are *not* present – 'mayhem', 'destruction', 'chaotic', 'cruel' (p. 5) – we sense them lurking under the surface. It will transpire that Briony's life and character also conceal suppressed imaginative energy, which will be released with catastrophic results.

Briony's life is shown to be ordered and harmonious. It sounds dull, but as she hates disorder she appears reasonably satisfied with it. She enjoys social advantage, but there is nothing interesting in her life. The last line of the first paragraph, is ominous: 'None of this was particularly an affliction; or rather, it appeared so only in retrospect, once a solution had been found' (p. 5). It tells us that something will happen but it is cryptic. It is hard to imagine what it could be that made Briony's lack of secrets look bad in retrospect. It is tantalising, and gives the first hint of **narrative tension** after a slow start. Only much later will it become apparent that the fact that there were no real secrets or intrigues in Briony's life led her to fashion one out of the events and characters around her, with dire consequences.

> **CONTEXT**
>
> McEwan, like Briony, felt that he grew up as an only child because his step-brother and step-sister were much older than he was.

This passage goes on to introduce the theme of writing which will be central to the book. Although Briony's play has already been mentioned, it has not previously been clear that this is the latest in a series of compositions. The language of this passage suggests the insights of an experienced writer, though it also expresses the thirteen-year-old writer's dissatisfaction with her earlier work. Briony's embarrassment leads her to keep her writing secret until a work is finished, and her anxiety that she is revealing too much of herself will be familiar to anyone who has tried creative writing. Her assumption that people will think she is writing about herself is partly justified. The fact that Briony has had little experience of the world so far is not necessarily a hindrance: for details of human experience, all writers must look inwards, hoping that what they find has general applicability and will be recognised by their readers. Briony's subject matter in the **melodrama** is, however, far outside her own realm of experience. In her early writing she can, to a certain extent, start to imagine other people's lives through her writing, but she is a long way from imagining other people's psyches.

There is **irony** in Briony's worry that the reader would speculate about her representing herself because we later discover that this is indeed the older Briony writing about her younger self. There is irony, too, in the assertions that 'she did not have it in her to be cruel' (p. 5) and that her ordered life denied her any possibility of wrongdoing. Although Briony is not wilfully cruel, she turns out to be astonishingly thoughtless and inconsiderate and Robbie, misunderstanding her motives, does believe her cruel and even vindictive. She manages to create chaos and destruction through her urge to make everything neat – the very urge which supposedly prevents her from doing wrong.

Briony's desire for order and harmony expressed in the neatness of her room is mirrored in the pattern of her narratives, both her written fiction and her account of what happened on the island. Briony's habit of writing stories in which fates are resolved and 'the whole matter sealed off at both ends' (p. 6) demonstrates the impulse that will soon lead to disaster. It is because she tries to impose a similar balance on the events and characters of real life, moulding them to make a story, that her imagination is able to wreak such havoc on those around her.

TEXT 2 – PART ONE, CHAPTER 13 (PP. 168–9)

From 'As early as the week …' to '… would be put at risk.'

The extended investigation of the rape is compressed into a short, vital passage of reflection. Briony's doubts about what she saw are acknowledged, and we see the process by which these doubts were quashed or ignored at the time.

The image of the 'glazed surface' of her conviction with 'hairline cracks' (p. 168) recalls the Meissen vase, mended so that the cracks are barely visible. Both the vase and Briony's story will come apart again later. It recalls, too, the flaw in the bowl in Henry James's novel *The Golden Bowl* (1904).

In acknowledging that she did not really see Robbie, but 'knew' (p. 169) it was him, Briony falls short of admitting that she lied. As a child, she believed in her strange means of perception. Indeed, her mother has been shown to have a similar faith in intuitive knowledge. Sitting silently in the house, Emily feels and senses what is going on around her, and 'what she knew, she knew' (p. 66). Briony sees what she expects to see: 'The truth instructed her eyes' (p. 169). This is a motif repeated throughout the novel, but it never has such dire consequences as here.

Briony interprets events so that they fulfil a pattern she has seen and wants to complete. She believes that symmetry and common sense confirm what she knows and that this in itself is evidence. We have already seen that she hates disorder. She will not write about divorce because it is messy. She will not violate symmetry in her own stories, and does not like to think it can be violated in real life. She has already wondered how to use the scene at the fountain in her writing. Now she is going beyond using experience to form stories, and is using story to recast experience.

The passage is presented as though it is a mirror on Briony's reflections at the time, though clearly it has been refracted through years of guilt and analysis of what she did. The writing makes excuses for her as she might have done herself: 'What she meant was rather more complex …'; 'There were no opportunities, no time …'

> **CONTEXT**
>
> In *Northanger Abbey*, Catherine Morland gives this account of herself: 'It had all been a voluntary, self-created delusion, each trifling circumstance receiving importance from an imagination resolved on alarm, and every thing forced to bend to one purpose by a mind which … had been craving to be frightened' (Jane Austen, *Northanger Abbey* (Penguin Classics, 1998), p. 188).

TEXT 2 – PART ONE, CHAPTER 13 (PP. 168–9) continued

QUESTION
Briony writes *The Trials of Arabella* very much with Leon in mind, as a lesson in how to choose his bride, but ends up writing her novel as an act of atonement. To what extent can, or should, literature serve a purpose?

(p. 169). There is a childish image of scary things emerging from the quiet village, something frightening and powerful that had been waiting for this catastrophe. She is overly defensive, voicing a childish desire to avoid blame, but there is also a more adult point to this, examining psychological motives. Briony as a child was eager to please, afraid of upsetting people, scared to change her version of events because she was nervous of disapproval or getting into trouble. This is convincing, and prepares the way for the courage she shows later in deciding to retract her statement. The recriminations will be far greater if she changes it in the future. She feels foolish if she deviates from her story as older, more experienced people show displeasure; it is 'wise' (p. 169) brows that frown. This extended explanation generates some sympathy for Briony. It is easy to understand a person, especially a child, being afraid to disappoint people and to get herself into trouble.

The final image, of the 'bride-to-be' (p. 169) who has doubts before a wedding, prefigures Lola's wedding to Paul in Part Three. Did Lola have doubts? At the same time, it recalls the marriage-centred plot of *The Trials of Arabella* and the unsatisfactory marriages of the novel so far. Instead of the appealing, foolish nervousness the comparison might be expected to conjure up, any reflection on marriage as it is presented in *Atonement* would suggest that doubts are highly appropriate.

The passage concentrates solely on Briony's actions and reactions. Her excitement, her desire to find or impose a satisfying pattern on events, and her fear of alienating people by expressing her doubts are all given as reasons for her to remain loyal to her story. The great absence in all of this is Lola. Everything put in motion by Briony could have been stopped by Lola, and why it is not remains a mystery. Lola's is by far the worse crime. The fact that Lola's motivations are not discussed comes down to a question of ownership: 'It was [Briony's] story, the one that was writing itself around her' (p. 166).

TEXT 3 – PART THREE (P. 312)

'We found *Two Figures* …' to 'Development is required.'

Cyril Connolly's letter to Briony about the story she has submitted for publication comes before we know that Briony is the **narrator** of the entire novel.

Connolly's style has an informal tone with some personal engagement, but his language is studded with arcane words and turns of phrase. He is comfortable with the jargon and process of literary criticism, saying 'and so on' (p. 312) after listing some erudite and complex point. He is careful, too, to acknowledge that the commentary is not all his own work. He uses a striking, unusual and apposite image to indicate how Elizabeth Bowen's comments have been incorporated into, and have enriched, his critique of Briony's work. His throw-away use of the phrase, 'as it were, mulched' (p. 314), conveys his confidence and fluency in contrast to the strained and self-conscious writing of Briony. His measured style has a very polished surface, but hides some cutting criticism. It resembles some of the novels of the day that presented emotional turmoil beneath a bland and disengaged relation of events. It is an accomplished evocation of the voice of an intellectual of the time.

Connolly is very aware that he is writing to a young person. His first comment is that the story 'was arresting enough to read with dedicated attention' (p. 312). This may sound like damning it with faint praise, and he immediately defuses any such suggestion by adding 'I do not say this lightly', making it clear that this is in fact a compliment. But he is not going to be effusive; he is, after all, rejecting the story. He goes on to point out some aspects that he liked before touching on his concerns about the piece. This is a formula often used in the professional world when giving feedback on an employee's performance as it is encouraging to the person and makes them more receptive to the coming criticism.

Where Connolly is critical, he uses polite language that make his objections sound slight, though once the jargon and circumlocution have been cut through, his remarks can be quite disheartening. The comment about Virginia Woolf implies that Briony's writing is derivative, that she has failed to develop a style of her own. The

> **CONTEXT**
>
> This letter is one of three letters given in their entirety and central to the plot. Robbie's letter to Cecilia in Part One and Cecilia's letter to Robbie in Part Two are the others.

> **CONTEXT**
>
> Connolly's identity is indicated by the initials, 'CC', and his job as editor of *Horizon*. Using real historical figures in a novel is a device commonly used to blur or draw attention to the distinction between fact and fiction.

phrase 'attempts at characterisation' (p. 312) is patronising, saying that Briony has tried but failed to capture the **characters**. His lengthy list of the virtues of examining the 'crystalline present' (p. 312) suggests that he does not like the style. (This is his own term, used to convey the way in which the descriptive writing of Virgina Woolf makes a crystal-clear picture of a moment captured in time.) He says that it is better suited to poetry, that it presents 'stylised' thought processes and is useful for 'experimentation' (p. 312), another patronising point that suggests Briony is still learning and has sent him an experiment in composition. The implication is that the style is not likely to produce finished, mature works. Using the word 'vagaries' (p. 312), which means 'wanderings', makes it sound pointless and trivial. It appears that Connolly does not greatly like the 'unpredictability of the private self' (p. 312), a trait he shares with the younger Briony of Part One.

The image of 'the long grass stalked by the leonine yellow of high summer' (pure Virginia Woolf) (p. 312) conjures up a vision of a lion stalking through long grass, even though it means only the colour of a lion is present. It is so original and arresting that it is instantly recognisable from its use in Part One. This is the first clue that Briony wrote Part One (and indeed the whole of the novel) herself.

The letter is an odd interpolation in the **narrative** and, on a first reading, it is the first time the novel turns on itself. It gives us a slightly queasy feeling to be in the middle of a novel, reading a criticism of the novel itself. The sense of dislocation makes us pause to reflect on the process of writing and on the artificiality of the whole construct – the novel we have is the product of drafting and redrafting, criticism and adaptation. The words from Connolly, which we are reading here, have supposedly shaped the way the book has finally turned out. Connolly's point that the work would be more engaging if there were 'an underlying pull of simple narrative' (p. 312) has been addressed in that the episode with the vase and Briony's observation of it does now lead somewhere. This tale, like all of McEwan's fiction, has an irresistible narrative pull created by a sense of terrible inevitability that emerges from people responding, in character, to tiny accidents and choices.

> **CONTEXT**
>
> Many echoes of Virginia Woolf remain. For example, when Robbie is walking to the house for dinner, he reflects on his 'great hoard' of time, his 'unspent fortune' (p. 92). In *The Waves*, Jinny says 'I have fifty years, sixty years to spend. I have not yet broken into my hoard' (*The Waves* (Penguin Classics, 2000), p. 40).

CRITICAL APPROACHES

CHARACTERISATION

The characters in *Atonement* are central to its success as a novel. In this respect, it is quite a traditional work. How far we believe in and engage with the characters in a novel determines how convinced we can be by the narrative. The three central characters, Briony, Cecilia and Robbie, are clearly drawn with layers of complexity and levels of interaction that make them thoroughly well rounded. Furthermore, McEwan develops similarities between characters who are members of the same family, which make their relationships all the more convincing.

Characterisation comes across in this, as in most novels, from the actions and speech of the characters. An **omniscient narrator**, who turns out to be Briony, presents different centres of consciousness to portray the points of view of several characters, giving insight into their personalities. Where the same incident is related from two or more points of view, the accounts highlight differences in the characters' outlooks and personalities. Briony is not an impartial narrator as she has her own central place in the narrative and relationships with the other characters. As all characterisation is mediated through Briony, it is worth stepping back and examining her motives in portraying others as she does. For example, Briony's feeling of having wronged Robbie and Cecilia may make her overly generous in her depiction of them.

Sometimes characters comment on each other, which can reveal information about each of them. Emily Tallis, in particular, is given an extended passage in which she voices her opinions of several of the characters around her (Part One, Chapter 6).

> **CONTEXT**
>
> The novelist Henry James coined the term 'centre of consciousness' for the technique of presenting the action from the point of view of character while retaining a narratorial voice in the third person. *Atonement* uses this technique extensively as an aid to character development.

BRIONY

Briony is the central character of the novel and the main narrator. She appears at three stages of her life: as a thirteen-year-old girl, a young woman of eighteen and as an elderly woman of seventy-seven.

BRIONY continued

The young Briony has been largely neglected by her parents but has otherwise had a privileged early life. She likes to see herself as a writer, and is desperate for drama. Her family has indulged her literary attempts. Everything she sees or does becomes potential material for her stories, making her somewhat callous in relation to other people and their experiences. She wants to be the centre of attention, and has little concern for the feelings or desires of others. Briony's own verdict on her younger self (and so presumably what she is aiming to convey in her portrayal of herself) is that she was a 'busy, priggish, conceited little girl' (p. 367), though this is certainly not the whole picture.

In Part One, Briony is poised on the brink of adolescence, and is beginning to shun overly childish activities and demonstrations of affection. The dangerous mixture of a child's view of the world and the desire to be respected by adults and thought worthy of participating in their realm leads to disaster:

> At this stage in her life Briony inhabited an ill-defined transitional space between the nursery and adult worlds which she crossed and recrossed unpredictably. (p. 141)

From the very start of the novel, Briony's passion for writing is key to her personality, and to the development of the plot. Initially, this goes hand in hand with her thoughtlessness. She marshals her cousins into rehearsing with no consideration of how they might feel. She is equally inconsiderate in abandoning the play when she decides to give up drama and concentrate on the new direction she has identified for her fiction.

Briony is childishly callous in ransacking experience for her fictions. In imagining she might find the twins floating face-down in the swimming pool, 'She thought how she might describe it' (p. 156). Most importantly, she sacrifices Robbie to her desire for a fulfilling narrative, making him the protagonist in the rape with no consideration for the impact it will have on him and others when she has doubts about his guilt. The inability to put herself in someone else's position and imagine how it feels to be them limits her writing as well as making her unthinking in her treatment of other people. When she matures, she is able to imagine being

CONTEXT

'When I got to the end of *Atonement* I felt that Briony was the most complete person I'd ever conjured' (Ian McEwan, interview with Jonathan Noakes; Margaret Reynolds and Jonathan Noakes, *Ian McEwan: The Child in Time, Enduring Love, Atonement* (Vintage, 2002), p. 23).

someone else – she is quite right to say it was growing up that changed her mind. The change to being able to empathise with others brings guilt as well as creative success.

All the principal aspects of Briony's character come together in Part One, Chapters 10–13, to make the crisis of the novel not only possible but terribly inevitable. Her desire for drama leads her into a frenzy of excitement and panic over Robbie's potential to be a 'maniac' (p. 119). It is an unfortunate coincidence that the attack on Lola happens while she is in this frame of mind, and that Robbie has gone alone to search for the twins.

Her imagination rapidly convinces her that Robbie is Lola's attacker, and her need to be the centre of attention is satisfied by being the only witness to the crime. She pushes her doubts aside, certain that she 'knows' Robbie did it because it fulfils her wish for a satisfying, tidy narrative in which events are played out as they should be. She finds a villain who acts true to form and can be discovered and punished, just as he would have been in one of her own moral tales, and so 'the terrible present fulfilled the recent past' (p. 168). Any suggestion that she might withdraw her statement or change her position is met with hostility from the adults, and her need for approval and attention is then enough to make her adhere to her story and quash any doubts in her own mind.

Five years later, the Briony of Part Three has grown up enough to realise what a terrible thing she has done. She is admirably brave in her resolution to do something about it, but she is still only on the brink of adulthood. Poised on the opposite bank of adolescence now, she is still unsure and immature in many of her actions.

During the course of Part Three, Briony is forced to grow up more. The arrival of the horribly injured men at the hospital brings her face to face with real suffering and death. Not all her childishness is stripped away, though – she is naïve in her hope that Cecilia and Robbie can forgive her and that she can make everything all right in some way. She also has childish fantasies about being thought a spy as she makes her way across London.

CHECK THE BOOK

Michael Frayn's novel, *Spies* (2002), also set during the Second World War tells how two young boys, inspired by the atmosphere of suspicion at the time, allow their imaginations to run wild, with dire consequences for the adults involved. Like *Atonement*, it reflects on the problems faced by children in negotiating adult worlds.

We know little of Briony's life in the period between Part Three and the epilogue, increasing the sense that her crime has been her life's key event, and her atonement its main focus and driving force. She has been a successful novelist, she has married a French man (reminding us of Luc Cornet and his mistaken declaration of love), and her clothes tell us that she is wealthy. Her extended family shows affection and makes an effort to celebrate her birthday and her life, so she is clearly popular amongst them. In the face of dementia, she is not yet panicking, but appears poised and calm.

At the very end of the novel, Briony is passing out of the other side of adulthood. We see her always on the boundaries – of adolescence, of adulthood, and now of death. These are times for reflection and re-evaluation, and times when past actions are seen in a new light. She feels she has atoned for what she did, at last, and is 'at one' with herself, at least briefly. As memory loss takes hold her mind will disintegrate. She knows there can be no going back over her work again and so has completed her final draft of the book and atoned as far as she is able.

ROBBIE

Robbie is the second most important **character** in the novel after Briony. The whole of Part Two centres around him and is related from his point of view, giving plenty of opportunity for his character to be developed.

In Part One, Robbie is a confident young man, fresh from studying English at Cambridge and with his whole life spread out before him. Because he enjoys the patronage of Jack Tallis, he has the luxury of being able to change his mind about his future career, and he uses this luxury freely. After a degree in English, he first plans a career in landscape gardening and then turns to medicine which requires expensive retraining. Is he flighty and indecisive, or multi-talented and unable to choose how to channel his energies for the best? It is hard to tell: the range of opportunities available to him emphasises how much is lost in the closing off of his life and in his early death. His talent and determination to work hard are unquestioned, and he is already studying alone to prepare himself for medical training.

CONTEXT

'I was in love with Briony and all her mistakes' (Ian McEwan, interview with Kate Kellaway, 'At home with his worries', *Guardian*, 16 September 2001).

Robbie is decisive and active, attributes that are demonstrated in the way he writes to Cecilia when he recognises his feelings for her, and goes to dinner with the intention of confronting her. These qualities stand him in good stead in France, where decisive action and determination to take charge of his own destiny are essential to survival. In smaller details, too, he is prepared for France. He speaks French, and his skill at map-reading and his passion for walking make it possible for him to navigate a route to Dunkirk.

CONTEXT

After university, Robbie plans to walk in Afghanistan, a trip McEwan himself undertook after university in 1971.

Robbie's abilities, his physique, his intellectual prowess, his ease in company and with himself all make him attractive. He has always been generous and caring with Briony – the story of her swimming lessons and his response to her stupid action in throwing herself into the water demonstrate this. In France, too, he is generous and selfless. He and his companions stop to help others even when in a dire state themselves. They are compassionate in their treatment of the bereaved grandparents and the victimised RAF man. Robbie comes across as a genuinely good person, making it all the more terrible that he is imprisoned for a rape he did not commit. The only hints of callousness in his behaviour in France are when he feels himself drawn to the unfolding spectacle of the RAF man's beating which makes him 'Unpleasantly excited' (p. 251), and that he, like everyone else, walks on past the cries of the injured in the ambulances after the Stuka attack. In London, he has to suppress his aggression towards Briony and wants to kill Paul Marshall: 'He … was fighting off an emotion he did not want witnessed' (p. 343). These lapses are sufficient to keep him from unbelievable saintliness, but insufficient to taint him.

In Parts Two and Three, Robbie is shown as a mature man. Though sobered and made more cynical by his experiences in prison and in the army, he is fundamentally as honourable, generous, compassionate, and fair a person as ever. The anger that could have poisoned his character is focused sharply on Briony and the people who supported her story – it has not made him generally embittered, nor wrecked his personality. At the end of the meeting with Briony in Part Three, Robbie is able to suggest a way forwards, a path that could help her atone. It costs him immense effort, but he is able to contain his anger: 'His eyes were steady, and he had everything under control. But there were drops of sweat on

QUESTION
Consider the importance of war at home and abroad for *Atonement*.

his forehead' (p. 345). The older Briony also allows herself to have Robbie acknowledge a glimmer of understanding of her mistake. When Briony says that she saw a man Paul's height he says 'My height' (p. 346). It is both a warning against being certain again and a recognition of how an error can begin.

The main focus of Robbie's character is his love for Cecilia and his determination to survive for her sake – 'she was his reason for life, and why he must survive' (p. 209). Her love and his hope for a future with her sustain him through prison and in France. It is a powerfully felt erotic love as well as a deep romantic love. His extended recollection of their love-making in the library makes this clear. The intensity of feeling conveyed in it is sufficient to convince us of his love and desire for her enduring through the ensuing events.

Love, and the urge to survive, form the driving principles of Robbie's character in Part Two. But he has other attributes. His love for literature and art, born out in his eloquent language and graphic descriptions which have the quality of painting in words, fill out his personality. Like Briony, he has enthusiasms – in his case, art, literature, gardening, walking, medicine. These make real his potential to live to the full, and so increase the agony of his life being wasted in the barren environment of prison. Unlike Briony, Robbie is fully able to engage and empathise with others of any social standing, a compassionate man who is deeply embedded in the social fabric.

Robbie is the character given most introspection. We are party to his private thoughts more than to those of any other character. The younger Briony is handled with **irony**, which creates distance, and makes her character less likeable. Robbie is genuinely likeable, and we are given such unlimited access to his inner state that we **identify** and empathise strongly with him. This empathy is necessary not just for him to be a credible character but for the full impact of his wrecked life to be felt.

CECILIA

Cecilia has finished her degree at Girton College, Cambridge, and spent the summer at the family house, but is frustrated at her inactivity. She had expected everyone would be pleased to see her and keen to involve her in things, but in reality the time has been empty. She has decided to spend time in the family home not because she wants to but because of 'a vague notion that her family was owed an uninterrupted stretch of her company' (p. 20). This leads her to sacrifice her time to them, a gesture that she petulantly acknowledges they do not appreciate. Like Briony, she has a childish desire to be the centre of attention. She puts herself at the heart of domestic matters, imagining herself indispensable to the smooth running of the household. However, we know that she has been away during term time for three consecutive years, and despite Emily's ineffectual management, the house has not lurched from one crisis to another. She has an exaggerated sense of her own practical importance – 'She simply liked to feel that she was prevented from leaving, that she was needed' (pp. 21–2). She is in awe of Leon and will not stand up to her father, while her mother does not value her intellect. She is a realistic product of the low regard in which girls were sometimes held at the time.

At the start of the novel, Cecilia is also something of a snob. She assumes that it is social difference, and his desire to highlight it, that led Robbie to remove his shoes and socks before entering the house earlier in the week. We learn later from Robbie that it was out of concern for Polly who was cleaning the floor, and because he feared his feet were smelly. Consideration, not social awkwardness, motivated his gesture. Cecilia has over-interpreted his action, imbuing it with more significance than it has. Robbie's revelation of the mundane and generous reality reduces Cecilia in our eyes, making her look laughably priggish.

In Cecilia's liking for dramatic gesture we can see her family resemblance to Briony. She is greatly concerned about how she looks to others. It is Cecilia's determination to project an image of herself that leads to the accident with the vase. She repeatedly looks at her own current experience as though she is reflecting on it from some point in the future, concerned even about how she will look back on herself in memory. Like Briony, too, she forms ideas precipitately which she then sticks to with determination. She decides that Danny Hardman is guilty, with no more evidence than Briony had for deciding Robbie was guilty of the assault. Likewise, Cecilia infers that Robbie is conscious of his social inferiority and

CHECK THE BOOK

The influential post-modern art critic John Berger has described in *Ways of Seeing* (1972) how women often imagine themselves being observed and act or pose with a view to how others will see them. Cecilia acts with a keen awareness of how she appears to others and will look in memory.

interprets his behaviour in this light. She believes that he is punishing her 'for being in a different circle at Cambridge, for not having a charlady for a mother' (p. 27), and that this is the cause of the awkardness between them.

Cecilia is not as theatrical as Briony, but her concern with how she appears to others is related to her tendency to pick a role and then play it. In Part One, she sees herself playing the part of a sophisticated young woman of her era, recently down from Cambridge and bored with life in the country. She is anxious talking to her brother, presenting her news in the way she thinks best suited to the impression she wants to create. During the night of the crisis, she adopts a dramatic, tragic pose, setting herself apart, chain smoking and wringing a handkerchief. She stares at her family, 'unable to believe her association with such people' (p. 179).

The Cecilia of Part Three bears little resemblance to the awkward, slightly snobbish and self-important young woman of Part One. She has, of course, grown up. She has suffered – by being separated from Robbie, alienated from her parents, despising her once-loved sister and living the hard life of a nurse, which is now made harder by the influx of terribly wounded soldiers. In her life at this point there is no space for a spoilt, upper-middle class ingénue.

CHECK THE BOOK
Vera Brittain's *Testament of Youth* (1933) gives an autobiographical account of nursing in the First World War.

While Robbie has the whole of Part Two in which to project his character, Cecilia has a more shadowy presence, filtered through her letters. She shares the stage in the last chapter of Part Three, and is present in France in the form of her letter, but is not given the same space as Briony or Robbie. This increases the sense that she is an innocent bystander rather than a main player. She is fierce in her love for, and defence of Robbie, and plausible as a nurse, but there is nothing now of her love of literature and no mention of any other source of joy in her life. Her only enthusiasm is negative – to distance herself from her family and cut herself off from her former life and character. Her singularity of purpose is not unrealistic – it is typical of people who become passionately devoted to a cause or campaign – but it makes her a less appealing **character** to us.

Cecilia's new character perhaps suffers from being a projection of the older Briony's desire to mould her to her own purpose. Cecilia is passionately in love with Robbie still. Her devotion to him and certainty of his innocence has led to her isolation. Separated from her family, its wealth and her comfortable lifestyle, she has an air of heroic solitude. Her anger with Briony is fully justified, yet she remains calm enough to soothe Robbie when he is in danger of losing his temper and hitting Briony. Has the older Briony created the adult sister she would have liked to have had? We learn in the epilogue that Briony did not meet Cecilia before she died, so has no personal experience of her character as an adult. In the earlier part of the novel, she recreates the Cecilia she knew intimately, but in Part Three she has to conjure her up, imagining how she would be, given her earlier personality and the likely effects that events will have had on her. None of the younger Cecilia's faults is in evidence in Part Three. Perhaps writing her a near-perfect character for posterity is part of Briony's atonement.

LOLA

Lola's name is an abbreviated form of Lolita, the central character of the novel of the same name by Vladimir Nabokov (1955). Lolita – who is called Lola by her lover – is the twelve-year-old girl for whom the European intellectual Humbert Humbert develops an erotic obsession. In choosing the name, McEwan is suggesting that she is a potent sexual force, perhaps a tease, but certainly aware of her attractiveness.

Lola is keen to appear more grown up than she is. She dresses in as adult a manner as she can, and she uses **idioms** and behaviour copied from her mother in dealing with the twins. She resembles a caricature of an angry mother, grabbing Jackson's ear and using **clichéd** phrases 'How *dare* you say that' and 'You will never ever use that word again' (p. 57). She acts the grown-up, too, in chastising Paul Marshall for saying that he had read about her parents in the papers. She is patiently indulgent of Briony's **melodrama**, though she cunningly manages to take the lead role for herself. At the same time, she is still very much a child. She relishes the chocolate bar, and how annoying it must be for the twins that she has it and they do not. She joins in Briony's excited condemnation of Robbie's letter,

CHECK THE FILM

A film version of *Lolita* by Vladimir Nabakov came out in 1962. It was directed by Stanley Kubrick.

and it is she who comes up with the word 'maniac' (p. 119) to describe him.

It is never clear whether Lola might actually be a willing partner in the action with Paul Marshall. Briony's words at Lola's wedding suggest she may have been:

> Poor vain and vulnerable Lola with the pearl-studded choker and the rose-water scent, who longed to throw off the last restraints of childhood, who saved herself from humiliation by falling in love, or persuading herself she had ... And what luck that was ... to marry her rapist. (p. 324)

Even if she were willing, her young age means that Paul's act would still be criminal. The nature of Lola's own crime, though, would be different (and possibly worse). The evidence is ambiguous. Emily Tallis hears a stifled sound which she thinks is Paul and Lola, and both of them come to dinner with injuries. Paul has only a slight scratch, while Lola has extensive bruising and scratches which suggest that she was restrained. But the aggression of the sexual encounter between Robbie and Cecilia in the library makes vigorous sexual activity not itself a sign of abuse. Lola, too, makes no attempt to avoid further danger from Paul and is not obviously upset when Briony first finds her. She had made one breathy cry before Briony knew she was there and is not crying; what Emily heard in the nursery was a squeal of laughter – neither is particularly alarming.

Lola's marriage to Paul in Part Three comes as a shock. Lola may have conveniently fallen in love with her rapist to avoid humiliation and difficulties. Maybe she imagined herself in love with him from the start, or was so hungry for attention in the midst of her own domestic turmoil that she welcomed his attention. Lola may seize on the chance of letting Robbie take the blame as an easy way out of resolving an attack. Or she may regret what she has done and prefer this new version of events. In any case, Robbie is as much a victim of Lola and Paul as of Briony.

We see some events through Lola's eyes before the assault, but judge her most from how Briony and Emily Tallis view her. Emily is resentful of Lola and sees in her many of the aspects of her own sister, Hermione, whom she dislikes. Her view that Lola is

CHECK THE BOOK

In *A Passage to India*, by E. M. Forster, the white girl Adela Quested makes a false accusation of attempted rape against the Indian character Dr Aziz. There are interesting parallels with *Atonement*. Adela suffers a traumatic experience of some kind while visiting caves, and Aziz, as an Indian, is less likely to be believed than Adela – just as Robbie is less likely to be believed than Lola.

attention-seeking, demanding, prone to drama and selfish is over-critical. We do not see Lola demanding much attention. She is quiet during the dinner, says little about the assault, keeps her injuries hidden from the adults and takes part in Briony's play without complaint. She tries to impress Briony with her maturity, but does not impose herself on anyone else. She is, if anything, overly compliant and so easy prey for Paul Marshall.

In Part Three, Lola is seen only as a bride and the object of Briony's thoughts. Her one act is to look at Briony and perhaps frown slightly. Nothing certain can be read into this. In old age, though, Lola is vigorous and robust, chic, steely and unassailable. Briony is certain that even if Paul dies, Lola will pursue a court case against her if she publishes her book revealing their secret. She has formidable energy and a 'terrible agility' (p. 358) which Briony senses comes from a deep sense of purpose, that of hiding her guilt and Paul's guilt. The rape, if rape it was, is part of a crime in which she colludes as well as being a victim. Lola and Paul are famed for their charitable patronage of many causes. There is a suggestion that this may be their way of atoning for what they have done, but it is of only passing interest to Briony. It is noticeable that the good causes Briony mentions all relate to interests of Robbie's – medicine, agriculture, and art.

PAUL MARSHALL

Paul Marshall is an unpleasant **character** from the time we first see him, but many characters in the novel do not recognise his failings. As he talks with Cecilia and Leon on the terrace, he reveals himself to be arrogant, conceited and to have a high opinion of himself and his confectionery business. The language in which his speech is related includes phrases that are clearly intended to be direct quotations from Marshall, giving an idea of his character and his view of himself. He has a grandiose view of what he does, describing how he has been 'for every waking minute of every day, enslaved to a vision' (p. 49). He appears quite ridiculous when it emerges that he has been managing the manufacture of a multi-coloured chocolate bar. He becomes even more self-important once he can include the war in his plans for the future: 'exhausted as he was, and maligned, he would not be turned away from his purpose, his vision' (p. 50).

> **CONTEXT**
>
> A total of over 53 million people died in the Second World War.

In keeping with his self-importance, Paul likes to be in control. He does not give the others much chance to talk, delivering a monologue about himself. He imposes his own will without regard for good manners, insisting that everyone try his chocolate-based cocktail even after Cecilia has diplomatically declined for them all the first time he offers it. If he touches Cecilia on the arm as they leave the terrace, which seems likely, this is another example of him imposing on others. Of course, he does this most forcefully in his assaults on Lola.

Paul is impolite and over-bearing in other episodes. During the dinner, he speaks first to Robbie, leaning across Cecilia to do so. Robbie winces at the rudeness of Paul starting a private conversation before talk is properly underway. His ostentatious gesture of tipping Hardman five pounds is vulgar and inappropriate as we feel sure he is not motivated by generosity. Though Paul is of a higher social class than Robbie, he has fewer social graces.

Paul is several times described as almost handsome, but his chin is too large and his features crowded towards the top of his face. He seems to consider himself handsome, however. It does not take Cecilia long to realise his limitations as she thinks how it might be to marry someone 'so nearly handsome, so hugely rich, so unfathomably stupid' (p. 50).

The most ominous aspect of Paul's character is his unpleasant sexuality. His erotic dream about his young sisters, and the lascivious way in which he watches Lola eat the Amo bar, prepare the way for his attacks on her. He is bold, certainly, to leave marks on her which will be visible at dinner and this suggests that he either considers he is above suspicion or does not see anything wrong in his actions – he is used to taking whatever he wants. When Briony comes upon Paul and Lola on the island, he does not run off, but skirts around the clearing before disappearing. He acts calmly, too, during the aftermath of the assault back at the house.

Paul's crime is not just sex with or rape of a minor, bad enough in itself, but to allow the innocent Robbie to be imprisoned for the assault. We are given no later insight into Paul's mind, and can guess at how he feels only from the few details of his later history that

CONTEXT

The value of a £5 note in 1935 was nearly forty times its current value, so Paul Marshall has given Hardman a tip of around £200 ($350 or 290 Euros) – a ridiculous amount.

Briony gives us in Part Three and the epilogue. He marries Lola: this is a certain way of keeping his crime secret, and closes off 'what *really* happened' (p. 371) to everyone else: 'the truth … was steadily being walled up within the mausoleum of their marriage' (p. 325). The marriage ceremony is uncharacteristically quiet and discreet. It is unlikely that this is just because of wartime shortages and austerity (they do have a Rolls Royce). It suggests that the marriage is a bit of an embarrassment, more an exercise in damage limitation than an expression of true love, at least for Paul.

In the epilogue, we discover that Paul and Lola have lived very public lives, often in the newspapers, defending themselves enthusiastically against any possible libel. They have made charitable donations to various causes. They live in fear of discovery and may feel guilty about what they have done to Robbie, though Briony does not openly reflect on this. Paul, old and frail, leans heavily on Lola; the image suggests that she now has the upper hand, that her response to the rape has been to hold him to ransom for the rest of his life.

Ironically, though Paul is morally undeserving of the social advantage he enjoys, he is ennobled, becoming Lord Marshall by the end of his life. It is a wry comment on the class system that a manipulative bully rises into the upper class through exploiting the commercial opportunity of the war, and that a rapist thus enjoys universal respect and admiration.

EMILY TALLIS

Briony's mother is noticeable by her absence from the first five chapters of the book. She has been effectively absent for most of Briony's life, and the task of looking after Briony, calming her after nightmares and cuddling her when upset, has fallen largely to Cecilia. Emily likes to think of herself as a committed mother, but her actions suggest the opposite. As the threat of migraine retreats in Chapter 6, she thinks of a host of other tasks she must carry out before she can go and search for Briony, even though she says this is the most important.

 CHECK THE BOOK

Henry James's short novel *The Sacred Fount* (1901) has a narrator who imagines that one character in a country house is drawing her strength from others. At the end it is unclear whether the **narrator** was mistaken or made it all up. The ageing of Paul and contrasting sprightliness of Lola echoes the situation in *The Sacred Fount*.

Emily is characterised by selfishness and inertia. She uses her proneness to migraine as an excuse for her absence from her children's lives and likes to imagine the difficulties that it has caused. She has an image of herself at the centre of the house, sensing all that is happening, but she does not actually engage with the household at all. Instead, she comes across as self-indulgent and lazy, a habitual invalid, constantly retreating before the threat of illness. She is trapped in her room, in semi-darkness, unable to live life to the full – but it is largely through her own choice. Her torpor extends to all areas of her life. She will not confront Jack about his affair and feels that they should not interfere in Robbie's life by paying for and encouraging his education – it 'smacked of meddling to her' (p. 151).

Although she likes to think of herself as a controlling presence, she is in reality completely ineffectual. She is not able to manage the domestic staff. She makes an inappropriate choice of meal for a hot day and is unable to back down. Betty is sarcastic to her, suggesting she make a bread and butter pudding salad, and it falls to Cecilia to find a solution to the problem. In fact, her children are accustomed to her uselessness and to humouring her: 'Whenever Mrs Tallis exercised authority in the absence of her husband, the children felt obliged to protect her from seeming ineffectual' (pp. 127–8). Emily does not either volunteer to look for the twins or phone the police as she does not grasp the gravity of the situation, seeing it instead as an extension of her sister Hermione's behaviour which she has so resented, and as significant mainly in being awkward for her. She assumes that everything and everyone is focused on her and is incapable of seeing any importance in events beyond their impact on her personally.

She would like to have another child and is already nostalgic for Briony's childhood. But it is her own lost position and eloquence that she mourns: 'she never spoke so well as she had to her eleven-year-old last-born' (p. 68). She enjoyed the feeling of easily-exercised power that being the mother of a young child gave her, folding her daughter with arms trapped in 'babyish helplessness' (p. 68), and of being of central importance to someone with no physical, emotional or intellectual effort. Now she resents rather than values Briony's growing independence and considers her daughter's talent a demon (p. 68). Her own view of life is jaded and she is dismissive of the idea that 'the weary, self-evident world could be re-invented by a child' (p. 68).

Emily's views are traditional and bound by both her class and the age in which she lives. She is conservative and superficial, seeing no point in Cecilia studying and believing that it will make her unmarriageable. She sees no value in knowledge that is not of practical use, and says that she does not want to know the scientific explanation for the behaviour of moths in being attracted to a flame – another demonstration of her unwillingness to disturb or go beyond the surface of things. She is snobbish, believing that it is not necessary for the family to be concerned with Robbie and his education, and seizes upon his supposed crime as evidence that she was right. Robbie comments later that she 'pursued his prosecution with a strange ferocity' (p. 227). For her to do anything with conviction is unusual.

However, in the moment of crisis, she rises to the occasion and takes charge. Cecilia is not capable or willing to act, yet Emily 'actually grew as her older daughter shrank into private misery' (p. 175). It seems that Emily's seclusion and status as an invalid suited the whole family and that they colluded in allowing her to preserve her inertia. When something else is needed of her – and events seem to endorse her view of the world – she is able to break free of her habitual role, and apparently sustain it, if Robbie's account of her zeal is to be trusted.

> **CONTEXT**
>
> McEwan has made scientific knowledge important and even central to his work in other texts and clearly does not share Emily's view. A debate about whether scientific knowledge was the antithesis of artistic appreciation of the world emerged in the nineteenth century.

LEON

Leon does not play a large part in the novel and, as we are not given any of the story from his point of view, he is presented only through other people. In the first part of the novel, Leon is filtered through Cecilia's adoration. Even so, the life she admires comes across as superficial and perhaps not as exciting as she imagines. He works in a bank, and spends his time rowing and seeing friends. He is relieved not to be promoted, and all the events he describes have happened to other people, not himself. The impression is of an easy-going man with no ambition or goals. He is undiscerning in his choice of friend: Paul Marshall is unpleasant and pompous, as well as being Lola's attacker. It seems that Cecilia is in awe of Leon because of their childhood relationship and because he is her older brother, rather than for any particular character traits or achievements.

However, Leon can take command of a situation when necessary. He can make the dinner run relatively smoothly, covering for his mother's social awkwardness, and he takes charge in speaking to his father when the twins disappear. In the epilogue we learn that he nursed a sick wife and brought up his children after her death, revealing latent abilities not apparent in Part One. He marries four times, which suggests that his easy-going, casual attitude continues, too. In his final appearance, at Briony's birthday celebration, he is in a wheelchair and paralysed on one side of his body. This echoes the division in his personality – one half lazy but one half competent and functional.

NETTLE AND MACE

As the two Cockney corporals with whom Robbie walks to Dunkirk are seen only from Robbie's point of view they have a tendency to blur into one. Nettle is the smaller, with a rodent-like face and protruding teeth. Mace is large and imposing. Their names are both the names of minor irritants: nettle is a stinging plant, and Mace is a brand of pepper spray used for personal self-defence (mace was invented in the 1960s but McEwan would be aware of its connotations for his twenty-first century readership). The two men irritate Robbie, though in fact they have their uses and are good men. Robbie feels responsible for them, but as soon as they join the main line of men marching to Dunkirk he thinks he has done all he is obliged to do and can lose them. He is wrong, though. Robbie needs their protection as much as they need his. His map-reading and navigation have been essential in crossing the countryside towards Dunkirk, but the corporals help and even save Robbie on several occasions. As Robbie's wound becomes infected, his mind wanders and his strength ebbs away. He depends increasingly on Nettle and Mace.

At the start of Part Two, Nettle and Mace annoy Robbie by teasing him about 'crumpet' (women) (p. 193). They seem more hardened to the horrors of the war than he is, since he dodges behind a wall to be sick after seeing the leg in a tree and it does not appear to affect them. But they are generous men. Mace stops to bury the French

CHECK THE BOOK

The play *Journey's End* (1928) by R. C. Sherriff (1896–1975) is one of the most famous depictions of the relationship between men thrown together as soldiers, this time in the First World War.

boy for his grandparents, even though he needs to keep marching and is already exhausted and parched in the hot sun. Mace comes to look for Robbie in the wood after the Stuka attack and gives him water. Mace also rushes through the crowd to rescue the air force man in the bar in Dunkirk, at considerable risk to himself. After a Stuka attack, they all stop to help the wounded, even the major who has just tried to recruit them to his mad scheme to flush out a German machine-gun emplacement. In the epilogue, Briony has letters from Nettle, who has helped her to piece together the journey to Dunkirk.

Nettle and Mace are more streetwise and shrewd than Robbie. They realise that Robbie looks likely to be pulled aside to man the perimeter defence outside Dunkirk and Nettle tells him to limp between them. They stop Robbie attacking the French civilian driver who annoys him, saying gently 'That ain't the enemy, Guv'nor' (p. 217), and they know to give the French farm brothers cigarettes, something that had not occurred to Robbie.

The two corporals have great faith in Robbie. His skill at navigating and his ability to speak French have seen them through to Dunkirk, but their trust is not just based on this, it is more instinctive. Nettle at first thinks Robbie is mad to agree to search for the old woman's pig (he is indeed delirious, and does it because he imagines the woman has some power to harm him). When the rescue turns out well, though, Nettle's trust in Robbie's judgement as something beyond his understanding but nonetheless good is restored.

THEMES

ATONEMENT AND GUILT

There are two crimes at the centre of *Atonement*: the attack on Lola, and Briony's act of bearing false witness. Only the second is of interest. The rape is a shadowy event, never clearly seen or investigated, and its consequences for Lola and Paul barely explored.

Briony's writing of the novel again and again is her act of atonement for her crime. The false accusation wrecks the lives of

 CHECK THE NET
The BBC website has a variety of resources on the Dunkirk retreat, from first-hand accounts to how it was presented in Britain as a victory rather than a defeat. Go to **www.bbc.co.uk** and type 'Dunkirk' into the search engine.

ATONEMENT AND GUILT continued

CHECK THE BOOK

The Rime of the Ancient Mariner, by Samuel Taylor Coleridge, tells of another crime and a lifetime of retelling it. A sailor shoots an albatross, an act that superstitious sailors believed would bring bad luck to a ship. He has the rotting albatross hung around his neck as a punishment, but everyone else on the ship dies. He is doomed to tell his tale to every third person he meets for the rest of his life.

Robbie and Cecilia, and for this Briony faces a lifetime of guilt. But how culpable is she? In her defence are her youth, her innocent (though foolish) motives and the lack of real opportunity she had to change or retract her evidence once adults had begun to act on her original statement.

Briony is not the only person who is guilty. Most obviously, Paul Marshall is guilty. Lola is guilty, too, in remaining silent about who attacked her. Lola finds in Briony's certainty a chance to escape the humiliation and difficulty of accusing Paul (or accounting for herself, if she was a willing partner). Paul and Lola let Robbie bear the punishment for Paul's crime and are more culpable than Briony – she at least believes he is guilty while they know he is not. It is possible that Paul and Lola try to atone through their acts of charity, but theirs is a different story, not the one which Briony is intent on telling.

Briony's family, the police and other experts involved in the prosecution must bear some of the guilt. The people who know her should recognise that her love of drama and her need to be the centre of attention make it very difficult for her to relinquish the position she has won by her certainty. Yet Briony cannot be absolved of all responsibility. When given the clearest chance, early on, to change her evidence, she refuses it: 'Yes, I saw him' (p. 181) she says, when the police officer tells her to disregard what she knows and think only of what she saw:

'You saw him with your own eyes.'

'Yes, I saw him. I saw him.' (p. 181)

Briony and those around her are not the only people who are guilty. Guilt extends through the novel, in the war, to the whole of society. At the end of Part Two Robbie, the most guiltless of characters, reflects on his own guilt. The Second World War was the most destructive event in human history. The span of the novel has seen 'First his own life ruined, then everybody else's' (p. 217). No one remains innocent:

What was guilt these days? It was cheap. Everyone was guilty, and no one was ... there weren't enough people, enough paper and pens, enough patience and peace, to take down the statements of all the witnesses and gather in the facts. The witnesses were guilty too. (p. 261)

Robbie feels guilty for the people he has not saved, the dead he has not buried, even though he realises that he could not save everyone. This does not mean guilt is not there, just that it is diffused. Everyone is guilty, by sins of omission if not of commission, of the war and its destruction of individual lives and society as a whole. It is a stark message of social responsibility, as relevant at the time when McEwan was writing as when Robbie is speaking. The fragile peace in Europe, patched together after the First World War, has been shattered. Guilt extends backwards in time, as well as forwards. When Betty is blamed for breaking Uncle Clem's vase, we know it was not her fault. It, too, had been pieced together inexpertly.

There are other small acts of guilt that are built into the larger picture of the novel and many of them are sins of omission, of staying silent. Emily is guilty of neglecting Briony and of neither searching for the twins nor calling the police; Lola is guilty of keeping silent; Cecilia is guilty of hiding her breaking of the vase; Robbie is almost guilty of doing nothing to save the RAF man, but is saved from this crime by Mace – an important act of redemption. (Indeed, Robbie is set apart from this general trend of guilt through inactivity by his tendency to decisive action.) The message extends to all of society, then and now: 'You've killed no one today? But how many did you leave to die?' (p. 261).

WAR

The Second World War is a presence throughout the novel even though it is most immediate and important in Parts Two and Three.

In Part One, the war is impending and casts its shadow over the action. It makes itself felt in the Tallis household through Jack's war work and Paul Marshall's hopes to cash in on any conflict by selling a camouflage version of Amo bars. It crops up, too, in casual references to Hitler and to the Abyssinian Crisis, creating a background awareness that casts an ominous shadow over the easy,

CONTEXT

McEwan has written and spoken extensively on politics and responsibility, including articles on the 9/11 attacks and the terrorist bombings in London in 2005 (see 'Only love and then oblivion', *Guardian*, 15 September 2001; and 'How could we have forgotten that this was always going to happen?', *Guardian*, 8 July 2005).

CONTEXT

The Second World War saw far fewer British casualties than Jack's department anticipates. There were 62,000 civilian deaths and 326,000 soldiers killed. France suffered similiar military casualties, but 470,000 civilian deaths. In Germany nearly 4 million civilians died.

pleasant lives of the Tallises. Emily dismisses Jack's statistics on likely casualties as improbably pessimistic, and the twins repeat to Paul their father's opinion that there will not be a war, but as readers we are aware of the war as historical fact. The life depicted in Part One is fragile, and the sense we have of its imminent destruction adds to its strange, elusive quality.

The first part of the novel is sandwiched between the First and Second World Wars. The First is present in Uncle Clem's vase and his own legendary heroism, in the disappearance of Robbie's father, whom Grace likes to think died in the war rather than simply ran off, and in the changed social hierarchy which has meant that Robbie and Cecilia have both been to Cambridge. The First World War reappears in the battlefields of northern France in Part Two, with the old woman who has lost a son and the French farmers bewildered at the return of the German army. Thus we see lasting effects of the previous war even as the Second World War is just starting.

The depiction of war in the second and third parts of the novel fleshes out the abstract numbers of Jack's report, realised in a sequence of horrific injuries and experiences that make us painfully aware of war's magnification of the same agony thousands of times over. Paul's plan to profit from the war looks particularly repellent when we see the suffering that has formed the foundation of his wealth. Parts Two and Three show the process of war from the point of view of soldiers at the front and war workers at home in England. The experiences of Robbie, Nettle, Mace and the people they encounter span a range from discomfort to agony. McEwan neither glorifies war nor ignores the more mundane suffering that was the lot of the majority of participants. Robbie and his fellow soldiers are disabled by blisters and bleeding feet, by exhaustion, hunger, thirst and aching wounds. These are not glamorous – they are the everyday torments often overlooked in depicting soldiers' lives but which make up the bulk of wartime experience. There are terrible bursts of violence, casually committed atrocities and transgressions against human decency, but the constant grind of marching and searching for food, drink and somewhere to sleep make up the major part of the soldiers' day.

Back at home, the nurses in England suffer routine discomfort from chilblains, hard work and emotional and physical exhaustion. The horror of the battlefield is seen most clearly in the injured hospital patients. During Robbie's journey through France, there has not been space to contemplate the detail of the wounds sustained by others, except by a few injured civilians, but here they are laid bare in all their horror. The agony for Briony and her colleagues is in seeing and dealing with these injuries. The nurses do good for the soldiers, but at untold cost to themselves. Their innocence, optimism and youth are lost to the war. No part of society is untouched, and no characters in the novel remain unaffected by the war. Even Emily, closed off in her private world of pain and privilege, bemoans the loss of railings and the evacuees disrupting life at the Tallis house.

In the epilogue, the war is embodied in the Imperial War Museum. Depositing the letters in the museum, Briony symbolically fixes the war in history. Yet in a novel in which the relationship between the past and the present is so closely examined, this locking away of a momentous past event is far from closing it off. The novel presents us with a sample of the myriad experiences that made up the political and military event of the war and demonstrates how the repercussions of these extend to the present time of the **narrative's** close; the war is certainly not over and done with in any final sense. Briony is wrong when she says that once all the people in her tale are dead their history will no longer be real. The letters of Nettle, Robbie and Cecilia are preserved in the museum and will bear witness to the past. Although Briony incorporates the old colonel's corrections to military detail, she is aware this is not really what is important about remembering a war. Its real history is in the lives and memories of those who have experienced it and the lasting effect it has on communities.

War, as it features in the novel, is largely about destruction and waste but it also about guilt (see **Atonement and guilt**, above). Its effects are not limited to its direct participants such as the soldiers and the nurses. The whole of society is guilty of allowing war to happen, allowing the type of suffering we witness in northern France and the London hospital. And the whole of society, too, loses out to the war – from the civilians killed in air raids or losing

CHECK THE NET

Go to the Imperial War Museum's official website for a history of the museum and lots of information on the Second World War: **www.iwm.org.uk**

WAR continued

CHECK THE BOOK

McEwan explored and responded to the threat of war erupting again forty years after the Second World War in the oratorio *Or Shall We Die?* (1983).

their livelihoods to invading enemy troops to the young women who lose their youth and optimism to the gruesome task of nursing the wounded. The war has lasting and wide-ranging social effects, too. Just as the First World War disrupted the strict social hierarchy that preceded it, so the Second World War has removed the last vestiges of that social structure. The new, post-war social order is exemplified in the West Indian taxi driver who confounds Briony's out-moded expectations and shows, perhaps, something worthwhile salvaged from the carnage. As Robbie has said 'the ploughing would still go on, and there'd be a crop, someone to reap it and mill it, others to eat it, and not everyone would be dead' (p. 235).

LOVE

McEwan has said that in writing *Atonement* he wanted to see if it was still possible, in the late twentieth century, to write a novel about love. *Atonement* is about many other things, too, but love remains a central theme.

Briony's family is largely dysfunctional. Emily says she loves her children, but it is an ineffectual love, never visibly resulting in any benefit or care. Briony and Cecilia love each other, but their love is squandered and destroyed by inappropriate actions. Cecilia adores and admires Leon at the start, but realises later that he is spineless and superficial. The only love left is the core love of Cecilia and Robbie, which nothing can alter. It is Robbie's love for Cecilia that keeps him alive in prison and in France. There is, for him, only love or oblivion.

It can be difficult to portray love, and especially tenderness, in a novel, without it becoming soppy, cloying or sentimental. McEwan avoids all of these. The change in Robbie and Cecilia's relationship from friends to lovers begins in awkwardness and antagonism. Their episode of passion is so intense it is aggressive, and the description of the sex astonishingly eloquent and sensual. But there is embarrassment, fumbling, and the interruption by Briony, which adds **bathos**. The lovers' heightened sensual awareness during dinner keeps the emotional charge and tension alive, extending it for hours.

By the time the lovers are seen together again in Part Three their love has the weight of worldly experience behind it and has been hard-won through years of waiting and suffering. It also has a purpose and immense strength. They have earned the right to compare themselves with the great lovers of history, recited in their letters. Cecilia's love draws Robbie back from the brink when he wants to hit Briony, just as it once used to bring Briony back from the brink of childhood nightmares. It is, Briony acknowledges at the end, unbearable that such love should not find its fulfilment. She cannot allow Cecilia and Robbie to die, as she suggests they did in 'real life', but makes their love transcend death by writing them a happy ending (or at least a happy continuation). Their love is not diminished in any way if they do not survive, but it is tragically wasted.

Is Briony being idealistic in bringing Robbie and Cecilia together happily, perhaps? We might wonder how much chance this relationship would really have, limited as it was to a single episode of interrupted love-making and then an extended correspondence from prison. McEwan does not avoid this issue, but confronts it head on in the tea Robbie and Cecilia share in London before he goes to war. But in the end it barely matters whether they could have lived happily ever after. Their story has become a fiction, but also an atonement and a tribute. As Briony says, they would soon all be forgotten anyway, without the book, and then what difference would it make what *really* happened' (p. 371)? The novel – hers and McEwan's – stands as a testament to love, and in that it deserves the ending which best suits its enduring purpose.

WRITING AND IMAGINATION

The process of writing is itself a central concern of *Atonement*. The novel is an extended study of its own composition, and includes its own shadowy history from a burgeoning idea, through critical input from the editor of *Horizon*, discarded drafts, the marshalling of evidence and the process of fact-checking to its final completion.

The novel is also about the making of a writer. Briony's earliest attempts at fiction are the moralistic tales she writes as a small child. It is when she witnesses Cecilia and Robbie at the fountain that the possibility of more sophisticated writing opens up for her. It is a moment of imaginative awakening, and a rite of passage. She feels

QUESTION
'Emotions have their narrative', McEwan has said. How does *Atonement* make a narrative of emotion?

that she is being initiated into an alien world that is impossible to understand, and certainly impossible to sum up in the simple, moralistic tales she has been writing:

> Briony had her first, weak intimation that for her now it could no longer be fairy-tale castles and princesses, but the strangeness of the here and now, of what passed between people, the ordinary people that she knew … (p. 39)

Writing involves more than imagining other consciousnesses, though. It must be a combination of story, **characters** and suitable style. Briony goes overboard in deciding to ditch story completely and follow the path of the **stream of consciousness** and impressionistic writings of the early twentieth-century modernists. In Cyril Connolly's phrase, she is in danger of 'throw[ing] the baby of fictional technique out with the folk-tale water' (p. 313). Although we do not get to see all of the story Briony has sent to *Horizon*, remnants remain, corrected, in the final version of the novel. This final version does indeed satisfy 'a childlike desire to be told a story, to be held in suspense, to know what happens' (p. 314) as well as showing us what it is like to be someone else.

As a young girl, Briony is only a writer in training. Language does not yet come naturally to her, so that she sometimes chooses inappropriate words and images. She wants order, a moral message and a pleasing logic in a **narrative** and does not consider unruly reality to be suitable subject matter. Divorce, she believes, is a 'mundane unravelling' (p. 8) that 'belonged in the realm of disorder' and was 'simply not a subject' (p. 9). Nor is she aware yet that the writer and reader must work together in the act of creation. The writer provides the starting material, but must release it for readers to build on. Briony complains that in performance her play has been 'defaced with the scribble of other minds' (p. 36), not realising that the involvement and cooperation of players and audience is the point of drama. All these points, though made through the portrayal of Briony's character, are points about writing as an activity and the role of the writer – of all writers, from the young Briony to McEwan himself.

By the end of the story, Briony is a successful novelist, and has written critically acclaimed works. But she writes and rewrites this one story throughout her life. It is the story that really matters to her, and the one that she must make sense of and take control of in order to make sense of her life.

Immediately before she sees the scene at the fountain, Briony has been wondering about consciousness, and the link between mind and body, intention and action. It is an important passage for the analysis of writing as well as of Briony's development. Briony wonders 'Was being Cecilia just as vivid an affair as being Briony?' (p. 36). She reveals that 'she knew it was overwhelmingly probable that everyone else had thoughts like hers' (p. 36), even though it makes her think the world unbearably crowded if two billion consciousnesses are operating as actively as her own. A novelist is in the business of making the world even more crowded, making new consciousnesses out of nothing. For Briony to succeed as a novelist, she has to be able to imagine herself fully inside the consciousness of another. She finally achieves it in presenting *Atonement* from the points of view of several of the characters – several centres of consciousness. We are convinced, reading Robbie's account of northern France, for example, that we can see it as he saw it. This infuses even trivial incidents, creating the psychologically real landscape of the novel. When Cecilia instructs Danny Hardman to take up Paul's suitcases, for instance, the older Briony has her wonder if he was interested in Lola (p. 48). This makes it credible, later, that Cecilia thinks Danny probably attacked Lola.

McEwan goes even further than this. In the older Briony presenting the younger Briony's account there are two layers of shift. The younger Briony, watching Robbie and Cecilia at the fountain says that Robbie 'imperiously' raised his hand (p. 38). This must be how it appeared to the young Briony, but the older Briony knows it was not an imperious gesture. McEwan gives the older Briony the ability to imagine herself into her younger skin – he is imagining himself into a **narrator** imagining another narrator imagining a third character's mind. It is like a nested set of Russian dolls, and a supreme achievement.

CONTEXT

McEwan has said that writing fiction is 'about showing the possibility of what it is like to be someone else. It is the basis of all sympathy, empathy and compassion. Other people are as alive as you are. Cruelty is a failure of imagination'.

CONTEXT

E. M. Forster is particularly good at placing tiny details that work as clues to, or justifications for, future events in his novels.

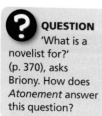

QUESTION
'What is a novelist for?' (p. 370), asks Briony. How does *Atonement* answer this question?

Atonement has a very real purpose for Briony. The question of the use or purpose of literature generally is raised at several points in the novel. In despair, Robbie thinks there is no point to it: 'What did the poets know about survival?' (p. 264). Yet literature sustains him, and when he imagines his future life it is filled with books, with the literature that makes him civilised and human. McEwan believes firmly in the moral value of literature and has said that being able to imagine oneself as someone else is the key to compassion.

TRUTH AND MEMORY

In the epilogue at the end of the novel, Briony says that there will always be readers who ask 'But what *really* happened?' (p. 371). In a sense, it is a meaningless question – like people who berate the stars of soap operas for the actions of the fictional characters they portray, these readers fail to draw the line between fiction and reality. In that, they resemble Briony's younger self. The novelist answers that what really happened is that the lovers live happily together – not because that is what happened in historical reality, but because that is what she has written, and so it is what happened in her novel. (In reality, of course, nothing happened as the entire novel has been made up by Ian McEwan. The very posing of the question makes us aware of this answer and points to the novel's status as artefact.)

CONTEXT
'I wanted to play with the notion of story-telling as a form of self-justification, of how much courage is involved in telling the truth to oneself' (Ian McEwan, interview with Jonathan Noakes, *Ian McEwan: The Child in Time, Enduring Love, Atonement* (Vintage, 2002), p. 20).

In the working out of the action of the novel, what is true is a central problem. It is not true that Robbie raped Lola, but it is, to a degree, true that Briony believed he did. It is not true that she saw him, but a lot hinges on her understanding of the word 'saw'. The police officer tries to clarify this, insisting on asking what she saw with her own two eyes. Briony is not to be let off on a **semantic** technicality – she lies about this. There are different types of untruth in the novel, with varying moral payloads. Lola and Paul are blatantly, undeniably, untruthful. Their guilt is so clear as to be uninteresting and is not explored. Briony lies about what she saw but is truthful about what she believed. But her beliefs have been moulded by her inability to separate fact and fiction, to choose what is too messy to be acceptable over what has an appealing **narrative** integrity. She fails to grasp that Cecilia and Robbie are more than just material for her writing; her imagination fails her and them as she cannot see what she is doing to the real people.

In a novel that claims to be constructed from events remembered from the past, memory is closely entwined with truth. Has Briony remembered accurately? If she has made up details, is she lying? Whether fiction is lies has a long philosophical history. Sometimes, she steps in as **narrator** and acknowledges that she does not remember: 'it was not the long-ago morning she was recalling so much as her subsequent accounts of it' (p. 41).

There are many lapses of memory and failures of understanding. The French boy, Luc Cornet, believes Briony is his French girlfriend. Briony answers his question by confirming that she loves him, as no other answer is possible and at that moment she does. It is both true and untrue. Robbie, delirious in France, imagines and recalls things that are not real. Emily wrongly thinks that Paul Marshall is good with children. Cecilia and Robbie are convinced that Danny Hardman was really the rapist.

But most importantly, Briony reveals at the end that she has vascular dementia and is losing her memory and other mental faculties. How reliable has she been as a storyteller? How much did she really remember?

In the epilogue, Briony also reviews the advice she has had about details of military history. She reflects that this type of minutiae is not what a novel is about: 'If I really cared so much about facts, I should have written a different kind of book' (p. 360). (Even so, she has corrected errors where to do so does not affect the fiction.) By raising this issue at all, McEwan makes us look closely at other details. There are many very tiny details that are accurate. There are also some that are so inaccurate as to alert us to the possibility that they are deliberately so. The page and illustration number are given for Robbie's copy of *Gray's Anatomy*, but they are wrong. The details could have been left out. Was it Briony who referred to a later edition than Robbie could have had, or McEwan? Perhaps most disturbingly, the description of vascular dementia is not entirely accurate. Is this evidence of confusion caused by the condition or an error? Briony's point that it is not the business of a novel to present detailed historical fact tells us how to judge *Atonement* in this regard. The truth it tells is a truth about, and distilled from, human experience and therefore immeasurably more valuable and important than tiny technical details.

 CHECK THE BOOK

At the end of *Enduring Love* (1997), McEwan invented a medical journal and an article describing a neurological condition he wanted to use, yet he employed a neurosurgeon to teach him the medical details required for *Saturday* (2005).

EVENTS AND THEIR AFTERLIFE

In many of McEwan's novels and short stories a brief event has vast, unimaginable consequences and completely changes the course of characters' lives. Because *Atonement* is Briony's attempt to account for and redeem herself, the unpicking of events is a central theme. The novel explores how such an event comes about as well as its consequences.

Part One presents in immense detail the process that leads up to the false accusation. There are many reasons that combine to produce the catastrophe – Briony's personality; the many coincidences that lead to Robbie searching alone, to Briony suspecting him of being a 'maniac' (p. 119) and to Lola being alone outside in the dark; the behaviour of the adults who make it so difficult for Briony to turn back from her assertion; Lola's unresolved motive in allowing Robbie to be blamed. Is it random or inevitable? Are the two mutually exclusive?

The causes and consequences of events wind through the novel. Often, the **narratorial** voice telescopes time to suggest how one thing might lead to another. As the dinner guests set out to search for the twins we lurch into the future to see how Robbie will reflect on his choice to search alone. The future intrudes again as Briony talks to Lola on the island and we see how she will reiterate her claim that she saw Robbie until it is unchangeable.

Witnesses to events are often wrong, as are their interpretations. Robbie wonders if Briony's childish crush on him lies behind her accusation; Cecilia thinks she and Robbie are awkward with each other because of their different social class. Different **characters** sometimes suggest different causes and even versions of the same event. There are many instances of characters (especially Cecilia) wondering about a moment, how it will look from the future, and what its impact will be. There are false futures anticipated, that spin off small narratives of their own. These prefigure the largest 'what could have been' of all, Part Three.

One effect of the tendency to look forward in time is to disrupt the **narrative tension** that depends on our desire to know what happens.

CONTEXT

At the beginning of *Enduring Love*, the narrator says 'I'm lingering in the prior moment because it was a time when other outcomes were still possible' (p. 2). The opening chapters of *Atonement* are extended in the same spirit.

Sometimes McEwan gives a hint of the future with sufficiently little detail to whet our appetite and increase tension. This happens at the beginning of Chapter 13: 'Within the half hour Briony would commit her crime' (p. 156). Elsewhere in Part One, it deflects our curiosity from what happens, on to how and why it happens.

In Parts Two and Three, the narrowed focus shows just what happened, with no attempt to tease out the significant events or explore how they might have a future life – the future is no longer important as the novel revolves around the false accusation. The ponderous consideration of events in Part One has given way, like so much else that characterises the first part of the novel, to a stark narration of what happened. The war is too enormous for the task of analysis to have any hope of success, and is the ultimate lesson in the senselessness of what happens. As Briony has said (p. 40), events have no meaning. Lola's marriage to Paul is inexplicable, and Briony makes no attempt to unpick it. It is another story.

CONTEXT

A line from *Twelfth Night* is relevant here: 'Thus the whirligig of time brings in his revenges', V.1.272–3.

The epilogue casts doubt on all that the novel appears to have said about events and their reverberations through history. The detailed plan of Part One accounts only for its own key point, the moment when Briony says 'I saw him' (p. 181). It does not secure a single path for the future. The future of Part Three is as plausible as that of the epilogue. The reversal – Cecilia and Robbie dying – undermines the **determinism** that Part One apparently promotes. The future cannot be known, but no more can the past.

LANGUAGE AND STYLE

There are many different voices in *Atonement*, which reveal the points of view of different characters. These voices are distinguished by the style of their language. Style includes the choice of vocabulary, the sentence structure and the use of imagery and **idioms**.

The language a character uses can tell us more about their personality or underline and reinforce aspects we have already seen demonstrated in other ways. The young Briony's point of view is put in language that reflects her literary aspirations and her keenness to add new words to her vocabulary. Her cousins are from the 'distant north' (p. 3), a phrase that recalls the language of children's stories; and divorce is the 'dastardly antithesis' (p. 9) of order, two words that she has clearly taken from a dictionary or **thesaurus** rather than come across in context. Briony enjoys words, but she suffers from a condition common in young writers of believing that a long or unfamiliar word is better (or cleverer) than a simple word. So marriage is 'nuptials' (p. 7) and the cousins' vivid hair colour is 'virtually fluorescent!' (p. 10). In relating events, Briony casts them into a story with literary self-consciousness, clumsily imbuing actions with weighty significance and giving too much overt explanation: 'Robbie imperiously raised his hand now, as though issuing a command' (p. 38). An experienced writer trusts his or her readers to interpret the action; the young Briony wants to keep full control of how her story is received. This reduces the role of readers and consequently their interest and engagement. Briony says later that she knows how to describe but not how to convey, and this is born out in her style.

Just as Briony's character is demonstrated in the style of language associated with her, so are the personalities of Robbie, Cecilia, Emily and Paul Marshall. Cecilia's style is packed with detail. It works hard to recreate a picture of events and environment. She did not just hurry across the park, but 'half ran' (p. 18) through a landscape itemised in detail. She uses arresting images created by unexpected choices of words: she has a 'blossoming need for a cigarette' (p. 18) and her ancestors are 'irretrievably sunk in a bog of farm labouring' (p. 21). Some of the images are apposite and evocative, some less so. We feel she is working hard at the style, and it is slow to read. Its intensity is quite exhausting, as even small details cannot be glossed over. For example, she describes the drawing room at length, even though she is only pausing to look at it. The 'south-east aspect [of the windows] had permitted parallelograms of morning sunlight to advance across the powder-blue carpet' (p. 20) and she catalogues all the things she can see – the faded Chesterfields, the 'almost new Gothic fireplace', the 'unused' music stands, and so on. Not only is there too much here that is not relevant, it is given an inappropriately vigorous life of its own. There is much personification with inanimate objects 'advanc[ing]', 'restrained' and 'permitted', making a busy scene straining with energy, that battles against the hot torpor of the day. There is no

CHECK THE BOOK

Cecilia's style owes a lot to that of Virginia Woolf, a point picked up in Connolly's critique of Briony's early draft. In particular, the style of *The Waves* (1931) and *To the Lighthouse* (1927) seem to inform Cecilia's intense and **lyrical** style. Woolf's essay 'Modern Fiction' (1919) set out her idea that the point of fiction was to present the internal life, a plan which allowed any amount of introspection.

possibility of working out which parts of the account might be important as nothing is given particular prominence. As a result, we concentrate at the same level to a stream of details that turn out to be of no great significance.

Robbie's style is easier, but in Part One it shares Cecilia's slow pace. He is more reflective, however. Instead of trying to recreate every detail of the scene, Robbie develops the important aspects in greater depth. Against Cecilia's literal and metaphorical dash through the landscape, which introduces her style, Robbie spends a paragraph recreating, vividly, the exact quality of the light and the changing sky as the sun sets (p. 78). He, too, speaks of a geometric shape of window letting in the light: 'Above him the framed rectangle of sky slowly shifted through its limited segment of the spectrum, yellow to orange, as he sifted unfamiliar feelings and returned to certain memories again and again' (pp. 78–9). Unlike Cecilia, he does not choose especially decorous or ostentatiously poetic language. He uses the language of everyday life and of science, with rectangles, spectra and segments. The description is given depth and relevance by its relation to his own internal state. This ties the writing together, giving a point to Robbie's observation which is missing in Cecilia's account.

We feel immediately that Robbie has more depth, that he can capture the world in language and she cannot do it as well. It is no surprise to learn that he earned a first class degree in English and Cecilia only a third.

In Part Two, Robbie's ability to pick out significant details becomes important. In northern France, there is too much to describe. A narration in Cecilia's style would overload us with information. Robbie helps us to feel what it is like by creating the details that make it real – his mouth and throat clogged with mud after the Stuka attack, or the feel of the sugared almonds the elderly lady gave him. The **juxtaposition** of details from normal life alongside the alien and horrific makes the war real – the terrible shreds of pyjama fabric near the leg in the tree, the farmer sheltering from the air raid as though from rain. The style is pared down, with no explanation of psychological action. Sometimes, a striking image is effective for reasons that are hard to capture. Robbie finds that his

CONTEXT

The use of everyday language rather than overly 'poetic' language was promoted by the **Romantic poets** William Wordsworth and Samuel Taylor Coleridge in the preface to the second edition of the *Lyrical Ballads* (1801).

'sugared almond tasted of [Briony's] name which seemed so quaintly improbable that he wondered if he had remembered it correctly' (p. 262). Not only the name, but the image is 'quaintly improbable', yet it works. It leads us to imagine the taste and feel of a sugared almond in an attempt to explore the image. Is it a strange type of synesthesia created by his fever, so that taste sensations are experienced as sounds? We all recognise the way that repeating any word robs it of meaning and makes it seem strange – the familiarity of this point carries us through the oddity of the comparison of the word with a sugared almond.

> **CONTEXT**
>
> The phenomenon of experiencing a stimulus of one sensory type as a feeling of another type is called synesthesia. A common example involves experiencing sounds as colours.

Feelings are created through the action and the language – Robbie's style achieves what the young Briony knows she must aspire to. When he goes to retrieve Nettle's boot, the language takes us through the approach to, and recognition of, the corpse. At first we, like Robbie, do not know what we are going to see: 'a black furry shape that seemed, as he approached, to be moving or pulsing' (p. 245). We share the gradual recognition with Robbie. First it looks 'furry', then as he (and we) approach it seems to move or, more precisely, pulse. Then the bluebottles become visible and the rotting corpse is 'revealed' (p. 245). Without using any but the most ordinary words, McEwan has recreated Robbie's experience of spotting something indistinguishable, puzzling over it, and seeing it resolve into a recognisable form, its gross reality uncovered with a stark shock. The impact of the experience is recreated in us, not described in Robbie.

On the rare occasions when emotion is openly expressed it is all the more powerful for its scarcity and the simplicity of the language used. 'Those poor bastards' (p. 257), Nettle says. It stands for the plight of everyone in northern France, everyone involved in the whole war, and is an understatement so breathtaking that it carries all the more weight. No effusive statement of the awfulness could be enough, but this works.

Briony's early style is analysed in detail in Cyril Connolly's letter. Although he is describing an earlier draft, traces of it remain in the finished Part One. The striking image of the 'leonine yellow of high summer', which Connolly commends (p. 312), survives into the current version (p. 38), linking the two versions like an umbilical cord. Connolly's criticism of the overly ornate, impressionistic prose must have caused Briony to cut down her description as the episode now occupies only a few pages rather than over a hundred. Even so, a lot of the language he compares to Virginia Woolf's style remains, especially in Cecilia's passages.

Briony's voice as **omniscient narrator** is fluent and neutral, carrying no obtrusive character and no emotional load, though she sometimes pauses to pass comment. She uses cool, measured language with an easy rhythm:

> Even without their attention and praise and obvious pleasure, Briony could not have been held back from her writing. In any case, she was discovering, as had many writers before her, that not all recognition is helpful. (p. 7)

This is assured but dispassionate prose, robbed of any emotional engagement by the passive voice ('could not have been held back'), the generalisation that places her with 'many writers before her', and the slightly dismissive 'In any case'.

In the epilogue, she steps out of her literary context and drops the voice of novelist/narrator to use a conversational rather than literary style:

> This, as they used to say, was the side on which her bread was buttered. That may sound sour, but it went through my mind as I glanced across at her. (p. 358)

It is a fluent, articulate and mature style. The easy use of the colloquial **idiom**, the direct address and anticipation of the reader's reaction create a sense of familiarity and intimacy that display a relaxed, confident relationship with language. Her need to control her readers' response is no longer paramount. She can now anticipate the reaction and disarm or redirect it gently, justifying herself. The novel has found its final voice.

> **CONTEXT**
>
> Cyril Connolly's own creative writings fell short of the promise he showed as a scholar at Oxford but he was extremely influential and talented as a skilled arbiter of literacy taste. As well as editing *Horizon*, he became principal book reviewer of *The Sunday Times*.

NARRATIVE TECHNIQUE AND STRUCTURE

Atonement is divided into three discrete parts and an epilogue, a structure that reflects movements in time and space and concentration on different **characters**. There is some symmetry to the pattern: we begin with all the characters together at the Tallis house, with attention concentrated on Briony. In Parts Two and Three, the **narrative** divides so that we concentrate on Robbie in France and Briony in London, with Cecilia a more or less shadowy presence in both. Finally, the stories come together again to end back in the family house, with Briony at the centre and the remaining surviving characters around her. It is not entirely symmetrical, though. Part One occupies half the novel's total length, and the epilogue only twenty pages. Further, the epilogue has a very different status. It reveals a **meta-narrative** – an outer fiction that encloses all that has come before. In stepping back from the story like this we find ourselves only in another level of storytelling, and one that moves the novel's preoccupation with the notion of truth to a new level of complexity and ambiguity.

The division of the main text into three parts allows McEwan to concentrate on key moments in time and place without the need to fill gaps or account for passing time. The novel could have been written very differently, showing how Briony came to feel guilty, how Robbie changed, what his life was like in prison, what Cecilia has done in the meantime. Instead, we see what happened and then are shown moments of what looks like **resolution**. It turns out in the epilogue that this is a misrepresentation.

Part One is quite different from Parts Two and Three in several ways. It is divided into numbered chapters, whereas the other parts offer continuous narratives with only slight pauses to indicate a change of scene or passing time. It is related from different points of view, whereas Part Two is told almost entirely from Robbie's point of view and Part Three and the epilogue almost entirely from Briony's point of view.

The multiple voices that crowd Part One also give this part its elusive, hazy quality. It is difficult to pin anything down – everyone sees differently, and for the greater part nothing much is happening

CONTEXT

E. M. Forster used the pattern of three parts, named after three places in his novels. *A Passage to India* is set in three places in India, and *The Longest Journey* in three places in England.

anyway. We see everything as though through a heat haze – shimmering, with indistinct edges. The real incidents are not seen head-on at all, but glimpsed or recalled later. We do not see the attack on Lola, only the aftermath in the dark. The fact that Briony, who relates it, does not see it is the key point. The other important episode, the love-making in the library, we also see it at its end, again in dim light, and then in Robbie's flashback.

Tiny incidents take on great importance in Part One because there is nothing else to concentrate on. The play, begun and abandoned, the broken and repaired vase, are the trivial details of everyday life. They are important momentarily to the people involved, but hardly the material from which great novels are built. But even these small events have their significance. The play, begun and then aborted, is finally produced in the epilogue, closing the novel by completing its very first action. The broken vase, rescued from the First World War, patched together between the wars but irrevocably broken in the Second World War could stand for all that the war has destroyed – the old Europe, innocence, a way of life.

CHECK THE BOOK

In Henry James's novel *The Golden Bowl* (1904) a flawed crystal bowl is similarly used as a symbol, and is smashed before the end of the novel.

The change to a single voice in each of the later parts of the novel gives them a more clearly defined focus. There is more action, and it is no longer hazy but right before our eyes – brutally so, in many places. Instead of being obscured by darkness or filtered through interpretations, we see events taking place as Robbie sees them in France. The leg in the tree comes as a shock to us, too; the darkened cellar is empty for us as well as for him until he sees the pinpricks of light made by cigarettes. We are carried along by the impetus of the action and the only moving backwards and forwards through time now is in his reflections and hopes. What happens is presented sequentially, at a steady pace that matches the relentless onward motion of his trudge to Dunkirk, although other characters suggest scraps of other stories going on around that could be told but are not. There is no time for other people's stories, and little space for compassion: 'Like everyone else, Turner kept going' (p. 242).

The novel expands its area of action as it progresses. From the claustrophobic concentration in the hot house and garden, it moves in Part Two to a journey through towns and countryside, and in Part Three to an extended area of London. The epilogue moves from London back to the house in the country.

CHECK THE BOOK

Epilogues or short additional notes at the end of novels are often used to tie the ends of a work together, achieving resolution and coherence. This is the opposite of McEwan's use of the epilogue. A good example is the 'Note' at the end of *Dracula* by Bram Stoker which replaces the trauma of the preceding chapters with a picture of perfect marital bliss. Stoker goes so far as to say 'Every trace of all that had been was blotted out' (Wordsworth Classics, 2000, p. 315).

The structure is deceptive. Before we read the epilogue, it looks as though the novel has presented an event and then the key points that lead towards its resolution: Robbie's survival in France and Briony growing up enough to face a meeting with the lovers where they will start the process of mending the damage done. The epilogue, by denying that this is what happens, wrenches the structure out of shape and pulls the two stories apart so that Robbie's ending and Cecilia's ending are split between parts of the novel and between England and France. The messy, frustrating lack of resolution is the very thing Briony tried to avoid in her childhood stories. Once again, she has used fiction to impose an order and rightness to events that they do not really have.

PART FOUR

CRITICAL HISTORY

Atonement is a very recent novel (2001). Although it has received much critical acclaim, there has been insufficient time for it to have become the subject of a body of criticism. It was reviewed extensively when it was published and received a few more notices when it was nominated for or awarded various prizes. In addition, McEwan has given several interviews and written articles himself on the subject of his life and work. These are the most useful for background information on the novel and on McEwan's intentions in writing it.

Reviews on the publication or nomination of a novel generally aim to give a flavour of the book and set it in the context of the writer's other works. The intention is to help readers to decide whether to buy or read the book. This makes them rather different from other forms of critical writing, which generally assume that the reader is already familiar with the text. It does not mean that reviews are necessarily superficial, but they give a broad sweep, indicating the main themes or concerns and the general character of the book. An excellent appraisal of the reviews and some more scholarly articles on *Atonement* is Peter Childs, *The Fiction of Ian McEwan: A Reader's Guide to Essential Criticism* (Palgrave Macmillan, 2006). Childs provides sizable quotations from some key articles and reviews, including those by Frank Kermode, Claire Messud, Hermione Lee, Geoff Dyer and James Wood.

Several critics have discussed the more obvious themes of the novel – love, writing, and imagination. Hermione Lee has also discussed how it explores a larger political topic in showing how twentieth-century society was shattered and remoulded by the Second World War and the events surrounding and following it ('If your memories serve you well ...', *Observer*, 23 September 2001).

Several critics have written of the relationship of *Atonement* to the work of other writers. Frank Kermode ('Point of View', *London Review of Books*, 4 October 2001, pp. 8–9) notices a superficial similarity to Henry James's *What Maisie Knew* (1897), a novel

CHECK THE NET
There is an up-to-date list of articles and books on McEwan's own website: **www. ianmcewan.com**

CHECK THE BOOK
Ian McEwan: The Essential Guide, by Margaret Reynolds and Jonathan Noakes (Vintage, 2002), offers a series of reading and thinking activities to help exploration of the text.

CHECK THE BOOK

The Work of Ian McEwan: A Psychodynamic Approach by C. Byrnes (Pauper's Press, 2002), looks at how McEwan's life has been reflected in his work.

about family turmoil and break up and the impact it has on a young girl. James's novel is told in the third person but from the point of view of Maisie, the girl. Geoff Dyer has compared *Atonement* to the novels of D. H. Lawrence in the way it exposes what lies beneath the veneer of polite upper-middle-class society, and to the writing of Virginia Woolf in its style. Dyer comments that 'McEwan seems to be retrospectively inserting his name into the pantheon of British novelists of the 1930s and 1940s' ('Who's afraid of influence', *Guardian*, 22 September 2001).

Earl Ingersoll ('Intertextuality in L. P. Hartley's *The Go-Between* and Ian McEwan's *Atonement*', *Forum for Modern Language Studies*, July 2004, pp. 241–58) has looked in depth at *Atonement's* relationship with *The Go-Between* and other texts. He examines not just the possible influences on McEwan but also the effect *Atonement* has had on our reading of other novels, including those written before *Atonement*. Making the point that the existence of *Atonement* alters a subsequent reading of *The Go-Between*, or even *Lady Chatterley's Lover*, Ingersoll draws attention to what a reader brings to a book and how our own prior experience and knowledge shapes what we find in it. This approach, following the lead of **postmodern** schools of criticism (see below), ascribes at least equivalent importance to the reader's response as to the author's intention.

ATONEMENT AND CRITICAL MOVEMENTS

Atonement presents an interesting case for critics because McEwan is aware of the developments in literary theory and criticism during the twentieth century and works some of them into his novel. As a writer self-consciously working within a tradition of **modernism, structuralism, poststructuralism** and postmodernism, he seems to have one eye on what the critics will make of it all. This makes the novel slippery and elusive; it touches on and plays with critical approaches, effectively undermining their attempts to grasp it.

CHECK THE BOOK

For a good, general guide to reading and discussing narrative using the tools of modern criticism, see Suzanne Keen, *Narrative Form* (Palgrave, 2003). It includes an excellent survey of major theorists and approaches.

The main movements in critical theory during the course of the twentieth century have been from modernism to postmodernism, incorporating structuralism, poststructuralism and **deconstructionist** theory. Parts of the postmodernist movement, such as **Marxist** and **feminist** criticism, concentrate on particular social angles in literature and its relationship to culture or society. Other areas concentrate on the relation of literary works to other texts and to the established forms of composition.

MODERNISM AND POSTMODERNISM

Modernism, broadly, encompass the unorthodox or experimental. Modernist fiction often dispenses with the linear 'realistic' plot, which formed the mainstay of nineteenth-century fiction and moves to a more fragmented approach to presented experience. Modernist writers tend to concentrate on mediating personal experience using experimental narrative methods and forms, often focussing on the alienation of the individual by society's structures, restrictions and expectations. While modernism overturns the ordered structure of the nineteenth century novel it does still intend to find and explore intricate, well-ordered structures of its own. Postmodernism, on the other hand, denies any order and allows unity to dissolve into fragments. Various meanings may emerge from the different organisation of these fragments, and by looking at elements in different **juxtapositions**.

It is possible to see reflected in Briony's development as a writer, and in the progress and structure of *Atonement* itself, the shift from conventional **narrative** to modernism and from there to postmodernism. McEwan could be mimicking the development of literary theory in microcosm in the approaches that he and Briony try out.

Part One follows a conventional narrative pattern, though takes a modernist approach in its style and insights into the psyches of the characters. Part Two develops the modernist trend further, with the only narrative action being Robbie's journey used as a canvas for reflection and a container for his **stream of consciousness** narrative, becoming increasingly experimental as his delirium disrupts any logic. Part Three has more narrative pattern, but this is set up for its reduction in the epilogue. The section combines elements of modernism and postmodernism. It explores Briony's mental state, and in Luc's delirious fantasising recalls that of Robbie in Part Two. The disjointed series of horrors seen through Briony's exhaustion, forms an intensely realised group of episodes set in an almost dream-like experience floating outside the realm of normal life.

CONTEXT

'There are surely no accidental word choices. McEwan's writing is lush, detailed, vibrantly colored and intense' (David Wiegand, 'Stumbling into fate', *San Francisco Chronicle*, 10 March 2002).

Cyril Connolly's letter introduces a postmodern awareness of the novel's own process of composition and this part of the book ends with Briony resolving to write the novel we have just read. The epilogue is thoroughly postmodern in its deconstruction of the whole of the preceding text and even itself. We have seen already how the epilogue unpicks the novel and forces us to think about the task of composition and the roles of writer and narrator (see **Detailed summary** on **London, 1999**). But this does not make *Atonement* an easy ride for a postmodernist critic. He or she would find their concerns reflected back at them by the text, which has already 'been there and done that'.

DECONSTRUCTIONALISM

The deconstructionist approach, which takes the novel apart to examine, almost forensically, the nature of its composition is essentially anti-narrative and anti-**mimetic**. Yet McEwan does not whole-heartedly endorse this attitude towards a text. He presents a challenge to this view, and to the question of what 'truth' there is in fiction, in Briony's overturning of the ending she has written:

'I can no longer think what purpose would be served if, say, I tried to persuade my reader ... that Robbie Turner died of septicaemia at Bray Dunes on 1 June 1940, or that Cecilia was killed in September of the same year by the bomb that destroyed Balham Underground station.' (p. 370)

Briony's difficulty forces us to reflect on the choice – the happy ending has provided a hundred pages of enjoyable and stimulating, coherent fiction; the 'truth' dismisses the lives of Cecilia and Robbie in a single dissatisfying sentence. We are likely to choose, with Briony, the fiction. In doing so, we become complicit in the deception, the preference for 'untrue', aesthetic story over dreary truth. The art of the novelist triumphs over the book's deconstruction.

READER-RESPONSE THEORY

The choice of ending highlights a distinction between texts of different types identified by the French critic, philosopher and theorist Roland Barthes (1915–80). He describes texts as being either 'readerly' or 'writerly' (or both). A writerly text involves readers in creating its meaning, requiring them to reflect on the method of its composition and the relation of its parts, to make choices and decisions and interpret rather than being restricted by a single meaning imposed by a dictatorial author. *Atonement* clearly falls into this category. McEwan highlights it for us by having Briony describe the history of its writing and Cyril Connolly comment on how it might be written before the current version is started. Briony herself begins as a writer of readerly texts with 'all fates resolved and the whole sealed off at both ends' (p. 6) and prefers that her creations are not 'defaced with the scribble of other minds' (p. 36). But she ends by undermining authorial responsibility and giving us the choice of which ending to prefer, or whether to hold both in uneasy tension.

The importance of what the reader brings to the text, both in terms of shared experience with the author and characters and in terms of individual ideologies, aspirations and experiences, is central to the reader-response criticism, or 'reception aesthetics', propounded by Wolfgang Iser (b. 1926) from the mid-1960s. Drawing on the model of anthropology, his is an essentially humanist doctrine in which the validity of any reader's response is equal to that of any other, whether or not it takes account of the social context of composition, the author's intentions (insofar as they can be discovered) or the work's position in, or relation to, the literary canon.

There are many strands within postmodernism which find meanings in a text relevant to, or informed by, different ideological positions. As a postmodern critic does not require meanings to have been placed in the text by the author, but discovered by the reader, from their point of view it would not matter whether McEwan himself shares any of the ideas raised through this type of reading.

CHECK THE BOOK

In *S/Z*, translated by Richard Miller (Blackwell, 1990), Roland Barthes offers an intricate dissection of a story by the French writer Balzac. Barthes demonstrates how language works on many levels in the construction of a fiction.

MARXISM

Marxist critics relate literary works to the social conditions that produced them and are reflected within them. A Marxist critic would find much to say about the social inequalities in the England of the 1930s and 1940s that led to Robbie's imprisonment. The impossibility the characters encounter in suspecting Paul Marshall as rapist is born of the English class system and makes Robbie's suffering almost inevitable, given the social context of the action. While a traditional Marxist critic would look at the reflections of social ideology in a text, a more recent Marxist would look at how social ideology is mediated by the text.

But *Atonement* was not written in the 1930s and 1940s, so the Marxist can also turn to the late 1990s and first years of the twenty-first century to find the social conditions which affected (or infected) McEwan as he wrote. The social and political conditions which have concerned McEwan include the aggressive dominance of the US in world politics, the social inequalities in European and American society and the way that prejudices relating to race, ethnicity or religion help to blind people to the humanity of others. It would be possible to draw instructive parallels between the conditions of anxiety and insecurity in the postcolonial UK and neocolonial US in the late twentieth century and conditions in the Weimar Republic and Europe between the world wars. A Marxist critic may ascribe to *Atonement* an intention to comment on the socio-political situation of the 1990s by refracting it through the lens of the 1930s and 1940s.

FEMINISM

Another thread in postmodern criticism is feminism. Feminist critics look at the representation of women in literature and the way this reflects and mediates social attitudes to women. With Briony as the central character, traced from childhood to old age, there is plenty of material for a feminist reading. In Part One of the novel, Briony is disempowered by the male and adult authority figures who do not deal appropriately with her, forcing her to stick to her original claim that she saw Robbie assault Lola. Yet ultimately Briony seizes back power for herself. She is empowered to reconstruct history according to her own perception and purposes

> **CONTEXT**
>
> '[McEwan's] initial, discarded notion about *Atonement* was as a futuristic novel in which the upper class was backward looking, as if living in the 18th century, and the working class reaped the benefits of technology. The hero, Robbie Turner, would have implants in his brain and mental access to the Internet' (Mel Gussow, 'A cool writer warms up', *New York Times*, 23 April 2002).

because she is in control of the novel's composition. This gives her an absolute role as creator, though she is somewhat uncomfortable with this. Briony might be considered to cast herself in a 'typically' subservient role in wishing to apologise or atone, something which she then finds is at odds with her role as the orchestrator of the action: 'How can a novelist achieve atonement when, with her absolute power of deciding outcomes, she is also God?' (p. 371). Is McEwan making a point about woman's inability to reconcile herself to this power, rather than just the novelist's difficulty?

METALANGUAGE

Such approaches tend to be partial, neglecting a large part of the text while mining it for nuggets that demonstrate one ideological concern. *Atonement* is very much a literary novel, and McEwan's concern with the text itself as an arrangement of words and structures is paramount. He explores it from the large-scale concept of fiction or story to the detail of individual words. *Atonement* includes not only a meta-narrative in the frame which the epilogue gives to the whole tale, but a metalanguage of its own in having both Briony and Cyril Connolly talk about its construction and its style. A metalanguage is one which provides a tool for discussing the language of the text itself. Postmodern critics would deny the existence of a metalanguage, but McEwan allows its possibility. At the same time, he explores the gap between words and their meanings which undermines the possibility, not just of a meaningful metalanguage, but of fixed meaning in any language. This gap was opened up by the early Swiss structuralist Ferdinand de Saussure (1857–1913) in separating the 'signified' (the thought intended by a word) and the 'signifier' (the sound of the word used for it). It became the territory of postmodern critics and theorists such as Jacques Derrida (1930–2004) and is colonised thoroughly by McEwan in making the meaning(s) of the word 'saw' central to *Atonement*: 'So when she said, over and again, I saw him, she meant it … What she meant was rather more complex than what everyone else so eagerly understood' (p. 169).

How the novel is put together and how it works, from the level of the metafiction to the ambiguous meaning of a single word, defeats any attempt to capture its potency using the tools of criticism. Perhaps this is why McEwan feels free to offer us these tools so

? QUESTION 'When a writer plans something new, and conceives a different kind of reader, he wants to … reveal to his public what it should want, even if it does not know it. He wants to reveal the reader to himself' (Umberto Eco, Postscript to *The Name of the Rose* (1983)). What type of reader does McEwan 'construct' for *Atonement* and what does he hope the reader will discover in him or her self?

METALANGUAGE continued

CONTEXT

'There are no hard distinctions between what is real and what is unreal, nor between what is true and what is false. A thing is not necessarily either true or false; it can be both true and false' (Harold Pinter, programme note to *The Caretaker* (1958); repeated in his Nobel Lecture, 'Art, Truth and Politics' (2005)).

explicitly. The novel remains more than the sum of its parts and no amount of scrutiny into how it was constructed ever reveals the magic that makes this particular combination of words into this particular triumphant fiction.

PART FIVE

BACKGROUND

MCEWAN'S LIFE AND WORK

CONTEXT
McEwan was one of the first students to work with Malcolm Bradbury on the famous and influential creative writing postgraduate course at UEA.

Ian McEwan was born in Aldershot, England on 21 June 1948. Aldershot is a main training centre of the British army, and McEwan's father was an army officer. His mother had two children by her first husband, a boy thirteen years older than McEwan and a girl ten years older. McEwan considered himself an only child. During his childhood, the family was posted with the army to Singapore, Tripoli and Germany. At eleven years old, McEwan went into a boarding school in Suffolk, called Woolverstone. After school he studied English and French at the University of Sussex and then enrolled on the modern fiction MA at the University of East Anglia. He spent part of the year after finishing his postgraduate degree travelling in Afghanistan and the North-West Frontier Province of Pakistan.

McEwan married Penny Allen in 1982 and they had their first son, William, the following year. The couple separated in 1998. McEwan won custody of his two sons after a bizarre and acrimonious legal battle during which his ex-wife kidnapped the young boy and her new lover appeared in court carrying a briefcase with Ian McEwan's name stencilled on it.

McEwan's first published work was a collection of short stories, *First Love, Last Rites*, in 1975. The tales draw on themes of unorthodox sexuality, violence and moral corruption. With his subsequent collection, *In Between the Sheets* (1978), and his first novel, *The Cement Garden* (1978), these gave him a reputation for being one of a new breed of 'dirty realist' writers who explored the dingy corners of the human psyche. The macabre continued to feature in later writings, but in the same way that Edgar Allen Poe (1809–49) used the extreme edges of human behaviour to gain a handle on the full spectrum of experience, so McEwan uses his explorations of the borders to illuminate the mainstream. In *The Innocent* (1989), set in Cold War Berlin, and *Black Dogs* (1992), which features dogs trained in rape by the Gestapo, normal behaviour and experiences slide almost imperceptibly into the bizarre.

In all McEwan's fiction there is a key moment, often an accidental or inadvertent event, which leads to the destruction of a life or of lives. It is a point from which there is no turning back, and from which a terrible and inevitable train of events unravels. In *The Innocent*, the central lovers – who seem to be perfectly ordinary people – find themselves carving up a dead body to hide it in a suitcase. In *The Child in Time* (1987), a man looks away from his young daughter in a supermarket and loses her forever.

The violence and sexual perversion which seemed gratuitous to some reviewers of McEwan's earlier fiction is maturely realised and fully embedded in *Atonement*. Paul Marshall – a maniac, to borrow Lola's term – is frighteningly recognisable and wholly plausible psychologically. He is all the more alarming for his apparent normality. The bloody destruction of the war, shown in searing detail, makes us feel as though we are being forced to watch, our eyes held open. There is a good deal of morality in this depiction of violence. McEwan has demonstrated a keen interest in politics, and the morality of the political regimes of the late twentieth century. He has spoken against nuclear arms and on the terrorist attacks on New York and London. The next novel after *Atonement*, *Saturday* (2005), continues the exploration of socio-political themes. Drawing from the terrorist attacks on New York in 2001 and set on the brink of the Iraq war (2003–4), it reflects on personal responses and responsibility for violence.

McEwan's work has been nominated for many awards and won several prizes. He won the Booker Prize in 1998 for *Amsterdam* and the Whitbread for *The Child in Time* in 1987. He was made a Companion of the British Empire in 2000, a recognition of a lifetime's achievements in British fiction.

CHECK THE FILM

Enduring Love has been made into a film directed by Roger Michell (2004) and starring Daniel Craig and Samantha Morton.

LITERARY BACKGROUND

Atonement is securely rooted in the traditions of nineteenth and twentieth century literature. It does not just draw on traditional forms, but uses them in a self-conscious way, playing with and combining them and drawing attention to them. The many references and **allusions** to other works which occur throughout *Atonement* (**intertextuality**) depend for their effectiveness on us, as readers, having some familiarity with the history of English literature. *Atonement* makes sense without this knowledge, but recognising the references gives the experience of reading the novel a richer texture.

The pattern of the whole novel mirrors very broadly the sequence of changing forms in English literature over the last one to two hundred years. Briony says of herself at thirteen, she has 'written her way through a whole history of literature … to arrive at an impartial psychological realism' (p. 41) and *Atonement* does something similar.

Part One has a conventional structure divided into separate chapters. It develops several characters and builds up to and then depicts an episode of crisis, a pattern familiar from the nineteenth-century novel. This part looks back to Jane Austen and Henry James in its carefully crafted plot and exploration of the consciousnesses of different characters. It draws on particular categories of novel, too.

The epistolary novel, or novel presented as a series of letters, is mentioned in Cecilia's reference to *Clarissa* and is present as a model throughout. Several important points of plot and character are presented through letters, and there is one important letter in each part of the novel. Also suffusing Part One is the tradition of the country house novel, in which the lifestyle, actions and interactions of the characters living in the self-contained microcosm of a country house form the focus. Overlapping with this is the tradition of the society novel, another model stretching from Jane Austen to the twentieth century. This embraces a body of writings from around the time Part One is set, including works by Evelyn Waugh, Rosamund Lehmann, Elizabeth Bowen, D. H. Lawrence

CHECK THE BOOK

The first notable country house novels were by Jane Austen. You could look at *Sense and Sensibility* (1811) or *Mansfield Park* (1814).

CONTEXT

The action of Part One is set in a single day, a device used by many writers and extolled by Aristotle as 'unity of time'. The most famous 'single-day' novel of the twentieth century is *Ulysses* by James Joyce (1882–1941). This presents every detail, humdrum and more important events, in the lives of three characters in Dublin. Like *Atonement*, it contains complex literary allusions and includes much trivia as well as some explicit sexual content.

and P. G. Wodehouse. These writers often adopted a wry, slightly detached or **mock-heroic** style which allowed sufficient distance to lampoon gently the upper-middle class lives they depicted. The language and style of Part One recalls the impressionistic writing of Virginia Woolf and other modernists (See **Critical history: Modernism and postmodernism**). Important models, too, are two novels in which a child's point of view of adult matters is a source of confusion and narrative development: L. P. Hartley's *The Go-Between* and Henry James's *What Maisie Knew*.

CHECK THE FILM

The anti-heroic depiction of the First World War in *All Quiet on the Western Front* (1930) shares the concerns of Part Two.

Part Two follows the consciousness of a single character, Robbie, showing changes of mood (including lapses into delirium), and moving backwards and forwards through time as he remembers and anticipates. It is introspective, concentrating as much on the internal 'events' of this part of Robbie's life as on what happens in France. There is little plot in the traditional sense, just a series of episodes that punctuates the monotonous walk to Dunkirk and the sea. The action of this part is summed up by Robbie: 'he was walking across the land until he came to the sea' (p. 219). Virginia Woolf is again a model, but this time in the structure and concerns of her writing. James Joyce is relevant for his **stream of consciousness** writing and D. H. Lawrence for his explorations of male consciousness and love. There is also a debt to poetry, with W. H. Auden and the poets of the First World War, amongst others, providing ideas and influence.

CHECK THE BOOK

Joseph Heller's *Catch-22* (1961), the most famous Second World War novel, presents a similar disillusionment and catalogue of horror centring on a single character's determination to survive.

Part Three is about Briony growing up and trying to resolve her difficulties with Robbie and Cecilia. There is action, but its importance lies in what it shows us about the process taking place within Briony. It owes a lot to the tradition of rites of passage or coming of age novels. There are many writers who have dealt with this type of subject – it is the mainstay of the English novel. The horrific depiction of the physicality of the human body to contrast with the inner workings of the conscious mind follows the pattern of the realists, evident also in McEwan's own early writings, particularly the short story collections, *The Cement Garden* and *The Innocent*.

The epilogue follows a **postmodernist** tradition in turning the spotlight on writing itself, examining its structures, purpose and process. Writers such as the Italian Umberto Eco, Argentinian Jorge

Luis Borges, Czech Franz Kafka and Americans Thomas Pynchon and Russell Hoban have been influential in pushing the boundaries of narrative in this way. This has been the concern, too of **poststructuralist** critics such as Roland Barthes and Jacques Derrida. *Atonement* does not go anywhere near as far as these writers, as it first presents a novel and then unpicks it. A closer model is *The French Lieutenant's Woman* by John Fowles which, like *Atonement*, offers two contrasting endings. This is also a novel that, up to this point, has followed a familiar pattern, exploring such issues as class, ethnicity, gender and sexuality.

McEwan, in his own historic setting, also belongs to the renaissance of the English novel in the 1970s and 1980s. A re-evaluation and flowering of the novel, opening up new themes and exploring previously-taboo areas, followed the social upheaval of the 1960s. McEwan stands with Martin Amis and Salman Rushdie at the vanguard of this change.

CHECK THE NET

www. themodernword.com is a comprehensive resource on postmodernist writers.

HISTORICAL BACKGROUND

THE SECOND WORLD WAR

The Second World War broke out in September 1939 when the German forces, under the direction of Adolf Hitler, invaded Poland. Britain and France had an agreement to defend Poland and declared war on Germany on 3 September 1939. Other European powers quickly became involved. The German army was better organised and better equipped than the Allied (French, British and Polish) forces. Using advanced tactics that worked by isolating and then obliterating portions of the Allied armies, the German army made rapid advances. The German air force was also better equipped than that of the Allied forces, with more modern planes that were strategically deployed to support the work of the ground-based forces.

French forces launched a counter-attack along a 100-mile stretch of the border between France and Germany, but this had little impact. Poland fell to the Germans on 27 September 1939, and the French recalled their troops, falling back to the Maginot Line on 13 September (see **Detailed summary** on **Part Two, pp. 234–46**). Most of the activity switched to the sea for the winter of 1939–40.

THE SECOND WORLD WAR continued

In the spring of 1940, Germany invaded Norway, then Denmark, and on 10 May began an assault through the Netherlands and Belgium with the ultimate goal of invading France. French defences were concentrated on the Maginot Line, but the Germans advanced through the hills and forests of the Ardennes, taking the French by surprise. The major German offensive came through Belgium, though, crossing the border on 12 May. The French had little in the way of defences in that region and the Germans advanced easily. The German troops swept quickly across northern France and turned, on 22 May, towards Calais and Dunkirk to cut off the ports through which British troops could be evacuated. It is against this backdrop that the British troops converged on Dunkirk in a chaotic panic at the end of May 1940.

The evacuation began on 26 May, by which time Calais had already been cut off by the German army. Because of German bombardment from the air and the destruction of the port's harbour on 27 May, it became impossible to land large ships to carry out the evacuation. The British navy pressed small craft into service, taking everything available, and used these to ferry soldiers from the beach at Dunkirk to the troop carriers waiting further out at sea. A total of 198,000 British and 140,000 French and Belgian soldiers were rescued by the evacuation through Dunkirk and more through other ports to the west.

SOCIAL BACKGROUND

ENGLISH SOCIAL CLASS

English society had a rigid class system for many centuries. Although the divisions had no legal foundation, it was difficult for people to move between classes. The class structure at the time of *Atonement*'s action was more rigid than it is now, although the terms upper class, middle class and working class are still in use to some degree today.

Class is based on socioeconomic distinctions. In the middle of the twentieth century, there were three broad classes in English society: the upper class, the middle class and the working class. The upper class traditionally comprised the nobility and landed gentry, and old families who can still trace their heritage back many centuries. They

CHECK THE NET

The BBC website gives access to a collection of material on the Second World War, gathered from the public. Go to **www.bbc.co.uk** and type 'people's war' into the search engine.

traditionally owned most of the land and, from the Industrial Revolution onwards, most industries. In the first half of the twentieth century, their wealth enabled them to lead privileged and leisured lives. They held most of the important positions in the political and military hierarchies. Their children were privately educated and often attended one of the oldest two universities in the country, Oxford or Cambridge.

At the other end of the spectrum, working-class people owned and earned little and worked in menial and often unskilled jobs, either in the factories of the towns and cities, in service (as servants) or on farms that they did not own. Robbie and Grace Turner are members of the working class, though Robbie's education has given him some social mobility.

In between, the middle class was a broad band of skilled, managerial and professional workers. If he had lived to become a doctor, Robbie would have been a member of the middle class. There were further divisions within the middle class according to wealth and profession.

The upper-middle classes, to which the Tallises belong, had acquired their money through some form of business – quite often banking or the legal profession. They enjoyed many of the lifestyle privileges of the upper class but less social prestige. Jack Tallis, as a senior civil servant, works at a high level within the government but has no personal power. He is not an elected member of government, and his job is to manage the execution of the orders passed down from government.

Traditionally, 'old money' – wealth handed down through the family – was considered more prestigious than 'new money' – wealth made recently through trade and industry. Paul Marshall, with his ambitions to make a lot of money out of manufacturing confectionery, would be considered vulgar. In giving Hardman a tip of five pounds, he is being ostentatious, another sign of vulgarity in English society.

The importance of class in *Atonement* rests on Robbie's status as a working-class person, and the tension that his social mobility has

> **CONTEXT**
>
> The University of Oxford was founded at the end of the eleventh century. It is thought that Cambridge University was founded twenty or thirty years later, around 1209.

ENGLISH SOCIAL CLASS continued

created. While Jack Tallis has recognised Robbie's ability and paid for his education, a charitable act which should have enabled Robbie to achieve a much better standard of living than would otherwise be available to him, Emily Tallis has a more traditional view, and believes that it was unnecessary and inappropriate to help in this way, and that her own children might resent Robbie being given the same chance as them (though this is clearly not the case). For Emily, movement between social classes is not to be encouraged. She enjoys the security of knowing that everyone is in their pre-determined social place and, as in other areas of her life, wants nothing to be challenged. When it appears that Robbie has raped Lola, Emily is angered at the abuse of the family's generosity but not surprised. Instead of judging Robbie's character, she sees only his social position; it is the type of behaviour she would expect of a working-class man, so she is content to believe he is guilty. Her ardent pursuit of his prosecution may be fuelled in part by her wish to put him back in his 'place'. Her snobbishness extends to anyone of a lower social rank than herself: '[PC Vockins] refused to display the deference one might expect from a policeman' (p. 146).

By contrast, Paul Marshall is beyond suspicion because of his social standing. The only other character considered as a possible culprit is Danny Hardman, another working-class boy. To prosecute Paul would have been very difficult. Had Lola really been raped by Danny Hardman or Robbie, it is inconceivable that she would have married her attacker.

In the army, too, Robbie's status is ambiguous. He is not an officer, but Nettle and Mace defer to him because he has useful skills (map-reading, speaking French) and has the education and social veneer of an upper-middle-class man, who would usually be an officer.

The changes in the class structure of Britain since the time when the novel is set are made clear in the epilogue. Briony's journey to the Tallis family home for her party is by taxi. The driver is Michael, 'a cheerful West Indian lad' (p. 362) who wants to play loud, thumping music in the car. If we make immediate assumptions about Michael, they are likely to be that he is from the urban working class – yet it quickly appears that he is a law graduate, now studying as a postgraduate at the London School of

CHECK THE NET

There is a series of photos of London during the Blitz at **www.historyplace. com**. Click on the 'Timeline of World War II in Europe' and then find the entry for 7 September 1940.

Economics, one of the most prestigious universities in the country.
Briony makes herself feel foolish by offering a trite analysis of a
subject about which Michael knows a lot more than she does. Any
expectations of class are immediately confounded. Michael drives a
taxi because he needs the money, but he is no less middle class, and
is better educated, than Briony.

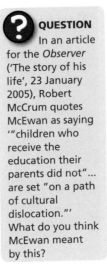

QUESTION
In an article
for the *Observer*
('The story of his
life', 23 January
2005), Robert
McCrum quotes
McEwan as saying
'"children who
receive the
education their
parents did not"...
are set "on a path
of cultural
dislocation."'
What do you think
McEwan meant
by this?

World events	Author's life	Literary events
		1747–8 Publication of *Clarissa* by Samuel Richardson
		1818 *Northanger Abbey* by Jane Austen published posthumously
		1896 *A Shropshire Lad*, poems by A. E. Housman
		1897 *What Maisie Knew* by Henry James
1914–18 First World War		
1919 Treaty of Versailles establishes the grounds of peace after the First World War		
1920 League of Nations comes into being; foundation of the Imperial War Museum in Crystal Palace, London		
1921 Adolf Hitler becomes leader of the National Socialist German Workers' Party		
		1922–39 T. S. Eliot (1888–1965) edits the *Criterion*

World events	Author's life	Literary events
		1924 *A Passage to India* by E. M. Forster
		1927 *Dusty Answer* by Rosamund Lehmann
		1927 *To the Lighthouse* by Virginia Woolf
		1928 Publication in Italy of *Lady Chatterley's Lover* by D. H. Lawrence
		1929 *The Last Summer* by Elizabeth Bowen
		1931 *The Waves* by Virginia Woolf
1935 Abyssinia Crisis – Mussolini invades Abyssinia and Hitler sends German troops to help the Abyssinians; the League of Nations fails to respond		
1936 Imperial War Museum moves to its current location in Lambeth		
1939 Outbreak of Second World War		**c. 1939–c. 50** Literary journal *Horizon* published

World events	Author's life	Literary events
1940 Collapse of Belgian and Dutch armies, invasion of northern France by Hitler; evacuation of British Expeditionary Force from Dunkirk and other ports; Blitz in London starts		
1945 End of Second World War; dropping of atomic bombs on Nagasaki and Hiroshima in Japan		
1946 Dissolution of the League of Nations		
1945–91 Cold War		
	1948 (21 June) McEwan born in Aldershot, Hampshire, in England	
		1953 *The Go-Between* by L. P. Hartley
		1955 *Lolita* by Vladimir Nabakov; *Catch-22* by Joseph Heller
1958–62 First wave of activity by CND (Campaign for Nuclear Disarmament)		

World events	Author's life	Literary events
	1959–66 Boards at Woolverstone school, Suffolk	**1960** Publication of *Lady Chatterley's Lover* is legalised in London
1969 British troops sent to Northern Ireland	**1967–70** Studies English and French at the University of Sussex	**1969** Foundation of the Booker Prize, the most important British prize for fiction
	1971 Creative Writing MA, University of East Anglia	
1972 (January) British troops kill 14 unarmed protestors; (February) Aldershot bombing, retaliation by the IRA	**1972** Travels in Afghanistan and Pakistan	
	1975 Publication of the short story collection, *First Love, Last Rites*	
	1976 *First Love, Last Rites* wins the Somerset Maugham Award; travels in USA; production of *Jack Flea's Birthday Celebration* (film)	
	1978 *In Between the Sheets* (short stories) published; *The Cement Garden* (first novel) published	

World events	Author's life	Literary events
	1979 BBC cancels production of *Solid Geometry*; finally filmed in 2002	
1980–9 Second wave of activity by CND	**1980** *The Imitation Game* produced for BBC's Play for Today series	
1980–91 European Nuclear Disarmament movement	**1981** *The Comfort of Strangers* published	**1981** *Midnight's Children* by Salman Rushdie
	1982 Marries Penny Allen	
	1983 William, his first son, is born; McEwan is included in the Book Marketing Council's Best of Twenty Young British Novelists	**1983** First Granta list of 'Best of Young British Novelists', featuring Ian McEwan
	1984 Elected Fellow of the Royal Society of Literature	
	1987 Wins the Whitbread Prize for *The Child in Time*; travels to Russia as a delegate for European Nuclear Disarmament	
	1989 Awarded honorary doctorate by Sussex University; *The Innocent* published	**1989** *London Fields* by Martin Amis

World events	Author's life	Literary events
	1992 *Black Dogs* published	
	1993 Film of *The Innocent*	
	1994 *The Daydreamer* published	
	1995 Separates from his first wife, Penny Allen	
	1996 McEwan's father dies	
	1997 *Enduring Love* published	
	1998 *Amsterdam* wins the Booker Prize	
	1998 Custody battle with his ex-wife for his two sons; McEwan wins custody	
	2000 Awarded CBE (Companion of the British Empire)	
2001 Attack on the World Trade Center in New York	2001 *Atonement* published	
2003 USA and UK invade Iraq for the second time		
2005 Terrorist bombs in London	2004 Film of *Enduring Love*	
	2005 *Saturday* published	2005 Harold Pinter wins Nobel Prize for Literature
	2006 Filming of *Atonement* starts: McEwan co-writes screenplay	

BOOKS BY IAN MCEWAN

First Love, Last Rites, 1975 (short stories)

In Between the Sheets, 1978 (short stories)

The Cement Garden, 1978

The Comfort of Strangers, 1981

The Imitation Game, 1981 (screenplay)

Or Shall We Die? 1983 (oratorio)

The Ploughman's Lunch, 1985 (screenplay)

The Child in Time, 1987

The Innocent, 1989

Sour Sweet, 1989 (screenplay)

Black Dogs, 1992

The Daydreamer, 1994 (children's novel)

Enduring Love, 1997

Amsterdam, 1998

Atonement, 2001

Saturday, 2005

FILMS

Enduring Love, 2004, directed by Roger Michell

ARTICLES BY IAN MCEWAN

There is a full list of articles on McEwan's website, **www.ianmcewan.com**

'How could we have forgotten that this was always going to happen?', *Guardian*, 8 July 2005

'Only love and then oblivion', 15 September 2001 (www.ianmcewan.com)

'Beyond belief', 12 September 2001 (www.ianmcewan.com)

OTHER WRITERS

Jane Austen, *Mansfield Park*, Penguin Books, 1994

Jane Austen, *Northanger Abbey*, Penguin Books, 1994

Elizabeth Bowen, *The Last September*, Vintage Classics, 1998

Sebastian Faulks, *Birdsong*, Vintage, 1993

L. P. Hartley, *The Go-Between*, Penguin Books, 2004

Joseph Heller, *Catch-22*, Vintage Classics, 2005

A. E. Housman, *A Shropshire Lad*, Dover Publications, 1991

Henry James, *What Maisie Knew*, Oxford Classics, 1998

D. H. Lawrence, *Lady Chatterley's Lover*, Penguin Books, 1998

Virginia Woolf, *The Waves*, Penguin Books, 2000

Virginia Woolf, *To the Lighthouse*, Penguin Books, 2000

FURTHER READING

CRITICISM

Margaret Reynolds and Jonathan Noakes, *Ian McEwan: The Child in Time, Enduring Love, Atonement*, Vintage, 2002

David Malcolm, *Understanding Ian McEwan*, University of South Carolina Press, 2002

Peter Childs, *The Fiction of Ian McEwan: A Reader's Guide to Essential Criticism*, Palgrave Macmillan, 2006

www.ianmcewan.com has links to reviews of and articles about his novels

BACKGROUND STUDIES

Malcolm Bradbury, *The Modern English Novel*, Secker & Warburg, 1993

Peter Childs, *Contemporary Novelists*, Palgrave Macmillan, 2005

Steven Connor, *The English Novel in History: 1950–1995*, Routledge, 1996

Dominic Head, *The Cambridge Introduction to Modern British Fiction, 1950–2000*, Cambridge University Press, 2002

Michael McKeon, ed., *Theory of the Novel: A Historical Approach*, John Hopkins University Press, 2000

Jago Morrison, *Contemporary Fiction*, Routledge, 2003

LITERARY TERMS

allusion an implicit reference to another work, a person or an area of experience the reader may share with the writer; allusion draws on shared knowledge

bathos moving quickly from an elevated topic or sentiment to a ridiculous, comic or banal one

canon the established body of literature

character a personality in a piece of writing who has consistent and developed personality traits

cliché a widely used expression which, through over-use, has lost any impact or originality

comic relief a pause in tension caused by the introduction of humour; comic relief breaks a sustained run of emotionally intense action

conceit clever or ingenious trick, such as an intricate idea or image given pleasingly imaginative expression

deconstructionist an approach to criticism which employs close analysis of a text in an attempt to unpick it and find a plurality of meanings within it. It is an application of **poststructuralism** which locates all meaning(s) within the text and does not make attempts to depend on outside influences

determinism a belief that the outcomes of action (or fate) are predetermined and cannot be altered by the operation of freewill on the part of individuals

dramatic tension sustained expectation or suspense which keeps the audience or reader anxious to know the outcome of an action or situation

feminist criticism criticism that seeks to describe and interpret women's experience as depicted in and mediated through literary texts

historical novel a novel set in a historical period, with the cultural, social, economic and/or political setting of the period playing a significant part in the development of the action and characters

identify (with a character) to emotionally align oneself with a character in a work of literature

idiom a word or phrase peculiar to a particular language and having an established meaning which often differs from its apparent or literal meaning

LITERARY TERMS

intertextuality explicit or implicit reference to other texts within a work of literature

irony wry humour derived from a discrepancy between words and their meaning, or actions and their outcome

juxtaposition the placing together of two or more, usually contrasting, ideas

lyrical originally meaning poetry intended to be sung, lyrical poetry expresses the emotions or thoughts of one person, often using language and rhythm that sound song-like. Lyrical prose is subjective, emotive, fluent and with features of poetic expression

Marxist criticism criticism which seeks to adapt the socio-political and economic ideology of Karl Marx (1818–83) to a reading methodology. After the Hungarian Georg Lukács (1885–1971), Marxist criticism concentrates on the depiction of social class structures, struggles and injustice. Marxist criticism relates the content of a work to the social shifts it represents or which produced it. More recent Marxist critics have concentrated on the 'gaps' in a text, and on what is left unsaid, as its more revealing aspects

melodrama a form of drama in which extravagant and sensational deeds and thinly drawn characters are portrayed, with strong elements of violence, sexuality and evil and a simplistic moral or judicial code

meta-narrative a narrative that is aware of it own status as a construct, often used as a frame for more traditional narratives

metrical feet an arrangement of syllables to give a particular rhythm to speech

mimetic relating to the convincing depiction or mimicking of reality

mock-heroic style emulating grandiose deeds, passions and personages, but used to present matter or character of slight importance or stature so that it parodies the heroic

modernism a move away from established structures and models to embrace the experimental and avant-garde in form and content

narrative a literary work that tells a story, or the progress of the action (story) in a literary work

narrative tension suspense created by the desire to know what is going to happen in a story or sequence of events

narrator the person or voice telling a story; an **ominiscient narrator** is a narrator who has access to all the viewpoints of the characters in the story, and tells it from a third-person perspective

parody a humorous, distorted or vastly exaggerated version of a literary form (or person, character or situation) which makes the model look ridiculous. Like caricature in drawing, it is a form of mimickry with the intention of deriding the original

popular fiction fiction that lays claim to no literary merit but which is written for a mass audience, often in a popular genre such as romance, crime, horror or science fiction

postmodernism a move into more radical and experimental forms of writing and criticism in which the forms and functions of literature are directly questioned within a work. Postmodern writing is often self-referential, and plays with the conventions and forms of established literature

poststructuralism a movement that finds fault with the premises of structuralism and tends to show that there are no definite and stable meanings in a text or even a word. It allows a plurality of views or meanings to coexist and denies the possibility of single, objective truth

reader-response a critical school which gives pre-eminence to the reader's contribution in constructing meaning in a text by means of what he or she brings to a reading of it

reflexive novel a novel which includes reflection on or attention to the method and process of its own composition

resolution events which form the outcome of the action in a literary work, with all problems, dilemmas and mysteries brought to completion

Romantic poet a poet writing in the tradition of Samuel Taylor Coleridge and William Wordsworth in the last years of the eighteenth and early decades of the nineteenth centuries. The English Romantic poets rejected the formal structures and ostentatiously poetic language of earlier poetry written in the classical and neoclassical traditions in order to write freely and subjectively about feelings, nature and personal experience using everyday language

semantic relating to the meaning of language and symbols

stream of consciousness writing which presents thoughts as they occur to a character or narrator with no overt attempts to link or structure them

structuralism a movement concerned with the methods of communication and the ways that meaning is constructed into signs (such as words). It finds that literature does not reflect a pre-existing and unique reality of its own but is a built up from other conventions and texts

sympathetic demanding or inviting our sympathy and engagement

thesaurus a book providing alternatives to words and phrases

tragedy originally a drama dealing with elevated actions and emotions and characters of high social standing in which a terrible outcome becomes inevitable as a result of a sequence of events and the personality of the main character. Classical dramatists in Greece and Rome and later European writers such as Shakespeare adhered to this model of tragedy. More recently, tragedy has come to include courses of events happening to ordinary individuals which are inevitable because of social and cultural conditions which could and should be changed. Writers of this type of tragedy include the Norwegian Henrik Ibsen (1828–1906), and Americans Arthur Miller (1915–2005) and Eugene O'Neill (1888–1953).

AUTHOR OF THESE NOTES

Anne Rooney taught English at the Universities of Cambridge and York before becoming a full-time writer. She has published over eighty books, including GCSE and A Level guides, and is a Royal Literary Fund Fellow at Anglia Ruskin University in Cambridge.

NOTES

Maya Angelou
I Know Why the Caged Bird Sings

Jane Austen
Pride and Prejudice

Alan Ayckbourn
Absent Friends

Elizabeth Barrett Browning
Selected Poems

Robert Bolt
A Man for All Seasons

Harold Brighouse
Hobson's Choice

Charlotte Brontë
Jane Eyre

Emily Brontë
Wuthering Heights

Brian Clark
Whose Life is it Anyway?

Robert Cormier
Heroes

Shelagh Delaney
A Taste of Honey

Charles Dickens
David Copperfield
Great Expectations
Hard Times
Oliver Twist
Selected Stories

Roddy Doyle
Paddy Clarke Ha Ha Ha

George Eliot
Silas Marner
The Mill on the Floss

Anne Frank
The Diary of a Young Girl

William Golding
Lord of the Flies

Oliver Goldsmith
She Stoops to Conquer

Willis Hall
The Long and the Short and the Tall

Thomas Hardy
Far from the Madding Crowd
The Mayor of Casterbridge
Tess of the d'Urbervilles
The Withered Arm and other Wessex Tales

L. P. Hartley
The Go-Between

Seamus Heaney
Selected Poems

Susan Hill
I'm the King of the Castle

Barry Hines
A Kestrel for a Knave

Louise Lawrence
Children of the Dust

Harper Lee
To Kill a Mockingbird

Laurie Lee
Cider with Rosie

Arthur Miller
The Crucible
A View from the Bridge

Robert O'Brien
Z for Zachariah

Frank O'Connor
My Oedipus Complex and Other Stories

George Orwell
Animal Farm

J. B. Priestley
An Inspector Calls
When We Are Married

Willy Russell
Educating Rita
Our Day Out

J.D. Salinger
The Catcher in the Rye

William Shakespeare
Henry IV Part I
Henry V
Julius Caesar
Macbeth
The Merchant of Venice
A Midsummer Night's Dream
Much Ado About Nothing
Romeo and Juliet
The Tempest
Twelfth Night

George Bernard Shaw
Pygmalion

Mary Shelley
Frankenstein

R. C. Sherriff
Journey's End

Rukshana Smith
Salt on the snow

John Steinbeck
Of Mice and Men

Robert Louis Stevenson
Dr Jekyll and Mr Hyde

Jonathan Swift
Gulliver's Travels

Robert Swindells
Daz 4 Zoe

Mildred D. Taylor
Roll of Thunder, Hear My Cry

Mark Twain
Huckleberry Finn

James Watson
Talking in Whispers

Edith Wharton
Ethan Frome

William Wordsworth
Selected Poems

A Choice of Poets

Mystery Stories of the Nineteenth Century including The Signalman

Nineteenth Century Short Stories

Poetry of the First World War

Six Women Poets

For the AQA Anthology:

Duffy and Armitage & Pre-1914 Poetry

Heaney and Clarke & Pre-1914 Poetry

Poems from Different Cultures

Margaret Atwood
Cat's Eye
The Handmaid's Tale

Jane Austen
Emma
Mansfield Park
Persuasion
Pride and Prejudice
Sense and Sensibility
Experience

Charlotte Brontë
Jane Eyre
Villette

Emily Brontë
Wuthering Heights

Angela Carter
Nights at the Circus
Wise Children

Geoffrey Chaucer
The Franklin's Prologue and Tale
The Merchant's Prologue and Tale
The Miller's Prologue and Tale
The Prologue to the Canterbury Tales
The Wife of Bath's Prologue and Tale

William Blake
Songs of Innocence and Experience

Samuel Coleridge
Selected Poems

Joseph Conrad
Heart of Darkness

Daniel Defoe
Moll Flanders

Charles Dickens
Bleak House
Great Expectations
Hard Times

Emily Dickinson
Selected Poems

John Donne
Selected Poems

Carol Ann Duffy
Selected Poems

George Eliot
Middlemarch
The Mill on the Floss

T. S. Eliot
Selected Poems
The Waste Land

F. Scott Fitzgerald
The Great Gatsby

E. M. Forster
A Passage to India

Charles Frazier
Cold Mountain

Brian Friel
Making History
Translations

William Golding
The Spire

Thomas Hardy
Jude the Obscure
The Mayor of Casterbridge
The Return of the Native
Selected Poems
Tess of the d'Urbervilles

Seamus Heaney
Selected Poems from 'Opened Ground'

Nathaniel Hawthorne
The Scarlet Letter

Homer
The Iliad
The Odyssey

Aldous Huxley
Brave New World

Kazuo Ishiguro
The Remains of the Day

Ben Jonson
The Alchemist

James Joyce
Dubliners

John Keats
Selected Poems

Philip Larkin
The Whitsun Weddings and Selected Poems

Christopher Marlowe
Doctor Faustus
Edward II

Ian McEwan
Atonement

Arthur Miller
Death of a Salesman

John Milton
Paradise Lost Books I & II

Toni Morrison
Beloved

George Orwell
Nineteen Eighty-Four

Sylvia Plath
Selected Poems

Alexander Pope
Rape of the Lock & Selected Poems

William Shakespeare
Antony and Cleopatra
As You Like It
Hamlet
Henry IV Part I
King Lear
Macbeth
Measure for Measure
The Merchant of Venice
A Midsummer Night's Dream
Much Ado About Nothing
Othello
Richard II
Richard III
Romeo and Juliet
The Taming of the Shrew
The Tempest
Twelfth Night
The Winter's Tale

George Bernard Shaw
Saint Joan

Mary Shelley
Frankenstein

Bram Stoker
Dracula

Jonathan Swift
Gulliver's Travels and A Modest Proposal

Alfred Tennyson
Selected Poems

Alice Walker
The Color Purple

Oscar Wilde
The Importance of Being Earnest

Tennessee Williams
A Streetcar Named Desire
The Glass Menagerie

Jeanette Winterson
Oranges Are Not the Only Fruit

John Webster
The Duchess of Malfi

Virginia Woolf
To the Lighthouse

William Wordsworth
The Prelude and Selected Poems

W. B. Yeats
Selected Poems

Metaphysical Poets